"I knew what the Dodgers represented

as a kid growing up in Brooklyn."

Joe Torre

{4220}

THE FINAL GAME AT EBBETS FIELD

...and other true accounts of baseball's Golden Age from New York, Brooklyn, Boston, Philadelphia and Chicago.

By Noel Hynd

Ebbets Field – Opening Day 1913

Third printing – October 2019

Red Cat Tales Publishing LLC
PO Box 34313
Los Angeles, California 90034

TYPOS: We hate typos as much as the reader. Maybe more. But you may find a small number. We hope we got everything correct. If you spot anything we missed, no matter how small, please let us know at the contact e-mail below, with TYPO in the subject heading. Corrections will be made for future editions on the day we are alerted.

Contact for typos, inquiries about photo usage and all other issues:
Red.Cat.Tales.Publishing@gmail.com

Photos and illustrations: all photos and illustrations here are public domain or fair usage, unless otherwise credited.

Special thanks to George Vecsey, Wally Exman, Joe Maglie, Larry Heyman, Carl Erskine, Jimmy Denny, Marc Weiss, Ralph Tyko of The Comfortably Zoned Network, Mike Shannon at *Spitball* Magazine, Patricia White, and artist Gary Cieradkowski. Also to Deb Jayne and Jeff Schatzki at SABR, for facilitating my attendance to the 2019 SABR bash in San Diego.

Some of the material here has appeared elsewhere in different forms, usually in shortened versions. I thank *Sports Illustrated* Magazine for helping facilitate material which originally appeared more than 30 years ago on the Red Sox great outfield of the 1920 era, the "balata" ball, the 1923 World Series, Carl Hubbell's incredible streak of wins, the "spite fence" in Philadelphia, the groundskeeper's apartment at the Polo Grounds, and "Lake Candlestick." A few topics also overlapped into *The Giants of The Polo Grounds.*

In memory, thank you to the players whom I had the pleasure of interviewing for those articles. Those gentlemen are no longer in this world. They include, Travis Jackson, Richie Ashburn, Marty Marion, Johnny Vander Meer, Dib Williams, Frenchy Bordagaray, Johnny Podres, Carl Hubbell and Doc Cramer, as well as non-players Robert Creamer, Art Rust., Jr., Lawrence Ritter and Matty Schwab. Thank you also to George F. Will for a prominent mention in *Men At Work* and to Jerry Schwab for some lengthy chats about the Polo Grounds many years ago.

BROOKLYN DODGERS
1955
VS.
NEW YORK YANKEES
★ ★ ★ 1955 ★ ★ ★
WORLD SERIES
GAME 1 PITCHERS: NEWCOMBE VS. FORD
SEPT. 28, 1955 - 1:30pm

"Go West, young man, go West and grow up with the country."

Attributed to Horace Greeley

New York *Tribune*

New York 1865

"I lived in Brooklyn for eight years, but it doesn't take that long to fall in love with the place. I did. Branch Jr. did. Our whole family did. We were devoted to the people, the Dodgers and the ballpark. Ebbets Field is now a memory, a lovable, cherished memory that makes a Brooklynite regret that so-called progress or the prospects of private profit can so easily grieve the public trust...

"It was a crime against a community of 3,000,000 people to move the Dodgers."

Branch Rickey (with Robert Riger)

The American Diamond: A Documentary of the Game of Baseball

Simon & Schuster,

New York 1965

"Oh, to be a center fielder, a center fielder—and nothing more!"

**Alexander Portnoy
in *Portnoy's Complaint* by Philip Roth**

Chapter 1 - The Final Game at Ebbets Field.

It happened on Tuesday, September 24th, 1957.

The sun had gone down over Brooklyn and the darkest night ever had descended on the borough.

Nonetheless, Ebbets Field, bounded by Sullivan Place on the south, McKeever Place on the west, Bedford Avenue on the east, and Montgomery Street on the north, glowed skyward from the seven irregularly arranged rectangular light towers that illuminated the field.

The eight national league flags on the roof flapped gently in a breeze in off the bay and the harbor. The grass was a deep green and the dirt of the infield a dark luxuriant brown. Outside the signs announcing the ticket prices - $3 for a lower box seat, $2 for grandstand, 75 cents for a piece of a bench in the bleachers - were still hanging. A heavy tarpaulin was on the field before the game.

A meager crowd drifted into the old ballpark and scattered around the thousands of empty seats. The 8:05 p.m. game time approached. It looked like the usual scene for an end-of-September game for a team that had dropped out of the pennant race. Except, nothing was normal. And nothing would ever be the same again. Dodger management would not officially admit what everyone in the park already knew. This evening's game against the Pittsburgh Pirates would be the last ever played by the Brooklyn Dodgers at Ebbets Field.

In the Dodger clubhouse before the game, the atmosphere was midway between subdued and morose.

"When I came here I heard that this was a tough town, that the fans could get on you," said manager Walter Alston, concluding his fourth season at the helm of the club. "But they treated me good. I'm slow making friends, but when I do, I hate to leave them."

"I don't think a ballplayer anywhere had better treatment than I've had in Brooklyn," said the team captain, Pee Wee Reese, shaking his head on the sadness of the occasion. "It's tough."

Everyone knew, in other words, that the deal was done.

There was a brief ceremony near home plate, the usual military representatives and local politicians. Representatives of The National Conference of Christians and Jews, a human rights organization focused on combating religious prejudice, gave awards to Gil Hodges, Roy Campanella and twenty-one-year-old Sandy Koufax. The NCCJ's origins could be traced back to 1924, when the convention for the Federal Council of Churches of Christ began to discuss the growing power of the Ku Klux Klan in America. As a result, a committee on goodwill between Christians and Jews was developed.

How could you *not* give an award to Gil Hodges? Hodges, an Indiana boy, had married a Brooklyn girl named Joan Lombardi. They made Flatbush their permanent home and raised their family there. He was regularly seen playing with his kids in Prospect Park and worked as an auto salesman at Brooklyn Century Chrysler. Would you buy a used car from a man like Gil Hodges?

Of course you would.

There was the perfunctory grounds rules meeting. The umpires were Augie Donatelli at home plate, Vic Delmore at first, Vinnie Smith at second, Jocko Conlan at third and for some reason, Ed Sudol in left field.

The starting lineups, announced by Tex Rickards. Time to pencil in the scorecard. Best idea to keep a running scorecard.

For Pittsburgh, Gene Baker leading off and at third. Roman Mejias batting second and in right field. Dick Groat, the shortstop, batting third. Fourth, Bob Skinner, the left fielder, Dee Fondy at first batting fifth. Bill Mazeroski at second hitting sixth. Roberto Clemente in center batting seventh. Hardy Peterson catching and hitting eighth. Bennie Daniels pitching and hitting ninth.

The Pirates were one of the weakest teams in the National League. The season had proven it. They were currently in a tight battle with the Cubs for the much coveted seventh place position in an eight team league. Yes, they had some solid players in the starting lineup, but beyond that they were weak.

And pitching?

"Friend and Law and that is all," might have been their little jingle about starters, their version of "Spahn and Sain and hope for rain." Tonight they had a young guy on the mound named Bennie Daniels making his first Major League start. Daniels had won seventeen games for Hollywood in the Pacific Coast League before being called up. This could be interesting.

And for Brooklyn, their last home line-up ever. It looked unusual to see the numbers and positions on the big scoreboard in right field under the Schaeffer sign:

Jim Gilliam would lead off and play second. Gino Cimoli would play center instead of Snider and hit second. Elmer Valo would play right instead of Furillo and hit third. Poor Elmer had played for Connie Mack's Philadelphia Athletics in the 1940's and then had landed with the Phillies until Brooklyn rescued him in the off season. Poor man. All those years in Philadelphia with crummy teams.

Where was I?

Gil Hodges was hitting fourth but playing third. Amoros, the man of the amazing catch in the World Series off Berra, he was out in left where he belonged, hitting in the five spot. Jim Gentile, a good looking young guy, maybe Gil's replacement someday, was hitting sixth and playing first. Roy Campanella was hurting, catching and batting seventh. Don Zimmer was at short and hitting eighth. Danny McDevitt would pitch and bat ninth.

Okay, so Campy and Hodges were starting, though Hodges at third base was an odd touch. Noticeably absent were Furillo, Reese and Snider.

Snider's season was said to be over. He had homered on Sunday and wanted his last at bat at Ebbets Field to be a home run. But Furillo and Reese were available. They were also due to play on the final three-day visit to Philadelphia that would end this horrible season the following weekend. Everyone knew the real dope, however: Furillo and Snider had knee problems. Pee Wee was almost ancient as he neared forty. Campy was coming off a lousy season: a doctor had nicked a nerve in Campy's hand during surgery. Jackie Robinson had retired after the team had tried to dump him to the Giants the previous December.

Danny McDevitt was completing a successful rookie year as a southpaw number four starter behind Drysdale, Newcombe and Podres. It didn't auger well for hitters tonight, but who knew?

12

Gladys Goodding, who had been playing the organ at Ebbets Field for nineteen years since being hired by Larry McPhail in 1938, played *The Star Spangled Banner* and sang it loud and clear as she always did. And the game was on. Missing, of course, was any official announcement concerning where the team would play the following year, even though Horace Stoneham's office had announced two weeks earlier that the New York Giants would be moving to San Francisco.

Equally absent was Walter O'Malley, the former team attorney who had made his first fortune as a bankruptcy lawyer during the Great Depression. He had become the Dodgers' team attorney in 1942 when Larry MacPhail resigned as general manager to serve in the United States Army as a lieutenant colonel. Over the years, O'Malley finagled himself into an ownership position with the Dodgers. He was now, more than anyone, seen as the one-man personal force for moving the Dodgers out of New York City.

Then again, why would Mr. O'Malley have been there?

Thirteen years earlier in 1944, he had gutted and rebuilt his parents' summer house out on Long Island and had relocated his family from Brooklyn to Amityville. The horror! There, as a pious family man, he attended church regularly and chaperoned his daughter's dances. On summer weekends he took the family sailing on his boat, which was named *Dodger*.

Not too far away, in Babylon, lived Robert Moses, head of the New York City Planning Commission and the man who refused to use taxpayers' money to underwrite a new facility for the highly profitable Dodgers. To say the least, they didn't socialize. The charge of "corporate welfare" was tossed around. Many Dodger fans really couldn't believe that the team would leave New York. But the majority of New Yorkers, even Brooklynites, took the attitude that if the team wanted to leave, O'Malley could take them. Branch Rickey would never have done this, it was widely said. But that didn't matter.

It also didn't matter that all year loyal fans had been wearing blue and white pins that said, "Keep The Dodgers in Brooklyn." The buttons, about 1 and a half inches in diameter, were created and distributed by the Keep the Dodgers in Brooklyn Committee, who had started a petition drive for a million signatures. The pins were handed out to fans entering Ebbets Field on opening day, April 19, 1957. On April 22, 1957 there had been a demonstration in front of Borough Hall to protest the Dodgers leaving Brooklyn. The pins had been all over the borough that summer and were in evidence tonight. They hadn't accomplished much. Walter O'Malley had even flashed one from time to time while making plans to uproot the club.

O'Malley didn't even own Ebbets Field anymore. The Dodgers had sold it to a real estate man named Marvin Kratter after the 1956 season and agreed to lease the stadium for three years. Meanwhile there was the issue no one wanted to talk about in public: as African-American attendance increased to watch Jackie and Newk and Junior, white attendance in the grandstands was on the *schneid*.

Vin Scully, Al Helfer and Jerry Doggett were in the radio and TV broadcast booth. The Dodgers took the field. Lovely white uniforms with royal blue trim and caps. There were many moist eyes in the thin crowd. It was like visiting a dying friend in the hospital; everyone was trying to be brave. Yet the grass still had that incredible greenness, as if Aunt Maureen had sent it over from Ireland. And there were the smells: hot dogs and mustard, cigarettes and peanuts. Wafting in from time to time was also the tantalizing smell of freshly baking bread emanating from the nearby Bond Bread Bakery that had been on Flatbush Avenue since 1925.

Danny McDevitt, a native New Yorker who would later pitch briefly for the Yankees, took the mound for the home team. He quickly retired Gene Baker, Roman Mejias and Dick Groat.

In the bottom of the first inning, Jim Gilliam walked for the Dodgers, took second on an error, then scored on a double off the right field wall by right fielder Elmer Valo. Gil Hodges and Sandy Amoros grounded out. The Dodgers had a 1-0 lead and Gladys Goodding sent another message and set the tone at the same time.

The lady seemed to be telling us something. She played *Am I Blue?* and *After You're Gone.*

It was easy to let one's memory drift. The ballpark was dark. It seemed to almost everyone to be darker than usual for a night game. Was management saving a few nickels on lighting upstairs? Who knew? And the game seemed very small compared with the events that reached out from history.

The park had opened with an exhibition game against the New York American League team in April 1913. Before the game, someone discovered that the flag, keys to the bleachers, and a press box had all been forgotten. Brooklyn played for real a few days later against the Philadelphia Phillies. A flag was secured and the keys were found. Brooklyn lost 1-0. A solid guy name Otto Miller was the catcher. Miller played thirteen seasons for the Brooklyns, including two World Series. He achieved a zany Dodger notoriety on October 10, 1920 in the World Series against Cleveland. He was the third Dodger tagged out by Indians Second Baseman Bill Wambsganss to complete the only unassisted triple play in the World Series. It *would* happen to the Dodgers.

The press box level at Ebbets was not added until 1929 but goofy stuff always seemed to happen there, stuff that didn't happen anywhere else.

In 1918 Casey Stengel, after being traded by Brooklyn to Philadelphia in the off-season, made memorable his return to Ebbets Field. In his first at-bat Stengel called time out, stepped from the batter's box and doffed his cap. A bird flew out and the fans broke into laughter.

A great hitter named Babe Herman once – or possibly more than once – set his clothing on fire by stuffing a smoldering cigar into a pocket. The same Herman, a ferocious hitter in his day, once hit what should have been a double but which instead instigated one of the strangest plays ever in baseball, one which involved three Dodger runners all standing on third base at the same time, looking confused and surprised to see each other.

"Babe Herman did not triple into a triple play, but he doubled into a double play, which is the next best thing," John Lardner wrote. The three-runners-on third incident (Babe Herman, Chick Fewster and Dazzy Vance) incubated a standard joke: a Brooklyn Dodgers fan, on being told that his team had three men on base, demands to know which base.

Later, the park's first night game was played on June 15, 1938, drawing a crowd of 38,748. Johnny Vander Meer of the visiting Cincinnati Reds pitched his second consecutive no-hitter in that game, a feat that has never been duplicated in Major League Baseball.

During these years, from 1920 to 1940, the Dodgers generally inhabited the second division, sixth place being a popular position, and acquired the adjective "Daffy," which was often hung on the team.

McDevitt worked quickly in the top of the second. He had a fastball that was starting to hum. Bob Skinner and Bill Mazeroski singled, putting runners at first and third after Dee Fondy had popped out to short. But Clemente hit into a double play: Hodges (at third, remember) to Gilliam to Gentile. Inning over. In the bottom of the frame, Zimmer and McDevitt walked, but were left on when Gilliam grounded out.

Between innings a platoon of white-clad hot dog vendors lugged steel trays around the tight aisles and narrow rows of the lower box seats. The franks had been boiled in a primitive kitchen under the stands, then packed onto trays that contained small vats of tepid water.

"Hot franks on a roll!" was the singsong call of a vendor, even this evening. The hawker was usually a kid from the neighborhood. On hot days and nights in summers the vendors would sweat into the water on the tray. No wonder the franks were so salty.

Watching the vendors was almost as good as watching the game. If the serving fork or the mustard stick dropped to the concrete, no hassle. No hassle and no hygiene, either. The vendor would wipe it off with a sleeve or a napkin or maybe a bare hand, the same bare hand that took the money – a frank cost twenty cents – and proceed with vending.

Sometimes a guy in the middle of a row would order a dog. The vendor would ask that the person seated on the aisle pass the frank along, with the expectation that the money would come in the opposite direction in a reasonable amount of time.

This lent itself to two particularly Brooklyn scams that usually victimized someone who stood out as a tourist. A vendor would pass the victim's hotdog down the row. As it went from hand to hand, each person took a bite, so that the smart guy who paid ended up getting a mustard-stained napkin and the appreciation of all the people in his row.

Other times a guy in a pass-along seat was slick enough to palm the entire dog - but not the bun - leaving the angry purchaser holding an empty hunk of bread. A lively argument would follow. Other fans would howl to the protesting vendor, who was going to come out short by two dimes in this exchange, to stop *#@!*% blocking the *@#!*! game.

Everyone knew too of the local Orthodox Rabbi, a pudgy benign soul, who used to hide in dark corners under the stands to munch Ebbets Field's very non-kosher franks. Many from his congregation had spotted him.

In the top of the third, Hardy Peterson, the Pirate catcher, singled. He was left on base.

In the bottom of the inning, Gino Cimoli, the Dodger centerfielder (Snider wasn't playing, don't forget) singled and moved to second on a groundout. Hodges singled sharply to right field and Cimoli scored. Scattered applause among the morose onlookers. The Dodgers were up 2-0. The inning ended.

Gladys Goodding's fingers settled on the keyboard again. She played a shmaltzy German song titled, *Don't Ask Me Why I'm Leaving*.

The Pirates went quietly in the top of the fourth. A walk, a strikeout and two groundouts.

In the bottom of the inning, Don Zimmer doubled to center for the Dodgers with two out. The next batter was the pitcher, McDevitt. A fine young man, perhaps, but he left Zimmer on second. Inning over. A vendor came by selling Borden's ice cream cups. He was not getting much business, even though Elsie was smiling on the label, just as she did all summer.

At the top of the fifth, Manager Alston made some changes. Jim Gentile left the game. Hodges moved from third to first. Pee Wee Reese came into the game, a last look at the Dodger great for the fewer than seven thousand people who were in the park. Applause! Reese played third. Campanella left the game. Joe Pignatano, a Brooklyn guy, replaced him. Piggie got some applause, too.

More memories flooded forward.

Durocher joined the team as a playing manager in 1938. He eventually gave up his part time job at shortstop so a young Pee Wee Reese could play. The Dodgers won their first pennant since 1920 in 1941. Leo kept the team fired up during the war years, almost always in contention. At the same time, Durocher made enemies everywhere he went due to his lifestyle, including the powerful Roman Catholic Archdiocese in Brooklyn.

Dick Young, the churlish sportswriter, described the way most people in baseball felt about Leo. "You and Durocher are on a life raft," he wrote in the *New York Daily News*. "A wave comes and knocks him into the ocean. You dive in and save his life. A shark comes and takes your leg. The next day, you and Leo start even."

In 1946, Leo ended up in court following a fracas in which he had punched out a noisy abusive 275 pound Dodger fan in a private room near the Dodger dugout. The fan had called him an unpleasant twelve-letter word that started with "m" and ended with "r." But it was Brooklyn and Leo was acquitted, partly assisted by some well-placed perjury from super fan Hilda Chester, whom Leo had befriended over the years.

Clemente singled when the fifth inning began but Peterson hit into a double play, Zimmer to Hodges. McDevitt whiffed the opposing pitcher, Bennie Daniels. Side out quickly.

Bottom of the fifth, a general lassitude overtook the park. Gilliam, Cimoli, Valo, three ground outs.

Top six, McDevitt was a young man on cruise control. A weak single to third for Groat. Pirates gone with nothing more. Bottom of the inning, more lassitude. Hodges, Amoros, Reese. World Series stars, but not tonight. The Daniels kid was throwing a sharp sinking fastball. Two pop flies and a grounder. *Sic transit gloria*. The defending National League champions were in third place behind St. Louis and Milwaukee, who had already clinched.

O'Malley was always jabbering about the situation in Milwaukee. Lou Perini, who owned the team, had moved an ailing Braves franchise from Boston. Perini used to be a construction guy with a lot of steam shovels. Now he was the owner of a ball club, setting attendance records every year. He had a date with the Yankees in the World Series, which is what the Brooklyn club normally had this time of the year. But what really rattled The O'Malley was that the new County Stadium, which the Wisconsin people had just about *given* to Perini, seated 43,000 delirious cheeseheads, had parking for ten thousand cars, and paid no city or real estate tax.

"How long can I compete with that?" Walter liked to ask people. "Not long," was the answer Walter wanted.

This young Bennie Daniels pitching for the Pirates this evening was from rural Alabama. But he had grown up in California. He was a vet of the Korean war, however, and had poise. He was doing fine. McDevitt was doing better. And Gladys Goodding was doing better than either of them.

As the game progressed, Gladys played, *How Can You Say We're Through* and, two thirds of the way through the game, *Thanks For The Memories*.

Top of the Seventh, McDevitt continued to bring heat. Good thing because the night was getting misty and chilly. Fondy, Maz and Roberto C. Three strike outs swinging. Danny McD now had six K's for the night.

Bottom seven, Zimmer singled with one out. McDevitt bunted him to second. Gilliam left him there. Through seven the Brooks were ahead 2-0.

People looked at the scoreboard. After more than four decades, two more innings in this *heimish* little place. Brooklyn had had a team since 1884, when they were part of the American Association. It was beyond sad. Remember all those crazy nut cases over at Times Square

20

with placards that read, "The End Is Near." They were right.

In 1947, a film had been released titled, *It Happened in Brooklyn.*

Sinatra starred in the movie, along with his pal Peter Lawford and Jimmy Durante. The story involved a Brooklyn guy, sort of an everyman, who had been in the war and had boasted to all his army pals what a great place Brooklyn was. Then he survived the war. No one more surprised than he! He came home and found that Brooklyn had changed a lot. Surprise again! But he meets a pretty girl, which was what every decent guy wanted to do along with root for the Bums. He wins her and everything is okay again.

All this was nestled neatly into a script with some attitude and an overdose of Brooklyn jokes. This was the era when the mere mention of Brooklyn on radio, in the movie theater or on television would elicit hoots, laughter and applause.

1947. Sinatra's film was ten years ago already? Brooklyn *had* changed a lot.

There were these big rock and roll shows now, proving to the wiser older generation of Brooklyn parents that these no-good kids these days would listen to anything. The music contributed to juvenile delinquency, you were told, and Aunt Sadie could tell you again if you were too slow to understand. Just earlier this month on September 5, a boy from Texas named Buddy Holly and his group the Crickets performed at the Brooklyn Paramount Theater at Flatbush and DeKalb. A loudmouth radio guy named Alan Freed was packaging shows featuring Holly along with Little Richard, the Del-Vikings, Mickey and Sylvia, Chuck Berry, the Diamonds, The Moonglows and Jimmy Rodgers. The place was interracial and usually packed.

Ebbets was interracial but wasn't packed. Attendance was still healthy while the Dodgers were in a pennant race. But the numbers had dropped every year since 1947.

There was television now, harness racing out on Long Island, and families moving to the suburbs where everyone owned a car. Nineteen Forty-Seven was also the year Jackie broke in and showed more courage than all the bigots who tried to make him fail. Leo was on Jackie's side.

"I don't care if he is yellow or black or has stripes like a…zebra. I'm his manager and I say he plays," Leo reportedly said, except he used a gerund that started with "f" in front of "Zebra" and everyone in Brooklyn over the age of eleven could quote it even though it was never in any newspaper.

Joe Black followed. So did Newcombe and Gilliam and across town at the Polo Grounds, Willie Mays, Hank Thompson and Monte Irvin, but the Jints didn't have any of them until Jackie, Joe and Newk were already in Brooklyn. Leo got suspended, came back, supported Jackie and then got fired again.

Meanwhile, the Brooks were on a roll. They won every national league pennant between 1949 and 1953, except for '50 and '51 and missed those by one game in each year. Then Podres pitched them to the only World Championship ever in '55, they won the flag again in '56 and tonight they were looking at closing Ebbets Field forever.

How could this have happened?

Gladys also knew it was crazy and sad. The organ music became more poignant, buoyant, misty-eyed but funereal at the same time, if such a thing is possible. She played, *When I Grow Too Old To Dream*, Nat King Cole's ode to aging love, *Que Sera Sera* (Whatever Will Be, Will Be) and perhaps most poignantly as the hours inched into the late evening, Bing Crosby's five-hankie tearjerker from

1933, *Where The Blue of The Night Meets The Gold of the Day.*

McDevitt struck out Peterson to start the eighth. Four K's in a row for McDevitt. Gene Freese batted for Daniels, who was finished for the season. Not a bad start. He would remain in the majors for seven more years.

Freese grounded to Reese at third, who - oops! - threw wide to Hodges at first, Freese reaching safely. E-5. You're scoring, right? Poor Pee Wee. The night was getting chilly. Not enough time to warm up. Plus he's a shortstop not a third baseman. And he's been playing since 1940. No matter. McDevitt fanned Gene Baker. Mejias popped out. Inning over.

ElRoy Face was pitching in the bottom of the eighth, all five feet eight one hundred fifty-five pounds of him, with the funny capital in the middle of his given name. A weird guy with a weird pitch, wouldn't you know? He threw a "forkball," a little known pitch which was hard to throw, hard to control, and even harder to hit. It was a change-of-pace offering that goes goofy. It gets its sudden drop because the pitcher jams the baseball between his index and middle fingers, allowing the ball to depart his hand with minimal spin. Properly delivered, it "tumbles" toward home plate, dropping out of the strike zone as befuddled batters futilely swing over it.

ElRoy was once asked if he knew where the pitch was going each time he threw it.

"I don't, but neither does the batter," he answered. Smart man, I guess.

Branch Rickey had once signed Face for the Dodgers. Then Rickey drafted him for the Pirates after Rickey abandoned the Dodgers to The O'Malley. Face had started games with the Pirates early in his career. Now he was the prototype of what would be the "closer" later on in the century.

The one pitch, one inning guy.

It was a cruel way to end the last game at Ebbets.

Cimoli fanned. Valo bounced out anemically to first, Face covering. That's 3-1 in your Ebbets Field scorecard.

Gil Hodges came to the plate. The last Brooklyn Dodger in Brooklyn.

Once, in what seemed like a lifetime ago in a giddier time but at this same arena, Hodges hit four homeruns and drove in nine in a 19-3 shellacking of the Boston Braves, before Braves flipped a finger to Beantown and left the city to the Red Sox who never won much of anything playing in the same league as the Yankees.

Maybe Gil would give one more thrill the loyal people who were standing and clapping in the left field grandstand. Gil tried. He struck out swinging. No souvenirs either tonight for the people out on the other side of Bedford Avenue, and there were a few gathered, as if outside a wake. Not even one ball into the glass above the scoreboard.

This horrible event ended with a whimper.

Groat flew out to Valo in right. McDevitt struck out Skinner swinging, his ninth. Then at 10:08 in the evening, Dee Fondy was the last batter at Ebbets Field. He hit a routine grounder to Zimmer at short.

Zim threw the ball to Gil at first and it was over. All over.

Tex Rickards, the gravelly-voiced announcer stuck to his usual postgame script. "Please do not go on the playing field at the end of the game. Use any exit that leads to the street." A bunch of kids ignored him, as did souvenir hunters, looking for grass or sod to keep. Tex was like the goofy uncle you liked but always ignored. And did anyone ever notice that Tex as starting to look a little like Wilbert Robinson, the old guy who managed the team in the 1920's and 30's, another genial fat guy.

In the press box it was suggested that Rickards update his announcement with the words, "any exit that leads to Chavez Ravine." But Tex stayed on script.

Gladys Goodding, from her glass enclosed organ loft above first base, pivoted from *Que Sera Sera* to *May The Good Lord Bless and Keep You.*

May there be a silver lining back on every cloud you see
Fill your dreams with sweet tomorrows never mind what
might have been...
May the good Lord bless and keep you till we meet again...

In the middle of this musical offering someone turned on the record player hooked to the sound system. Those moving slowly to the exits, or those staring unbelieving at an emptying field, got to hear the recording played at the end of every Brooklyn Dodgers game, appropriately named, *Follow The Dodgers*.

> *Oh, Follow The Dodgers,*
> *Follow the Dodgers Around*
> *The infield, The outfield,*
> *The catcher and the fellow on the mound....*

Then this too was interrupted. Gladys finished her recital with the more appropriate *Auld Lang Syne*. And Guy Lombardo was nowhere to be seen.

Alston was the last Dodger off the field. In the locker room, shock and sadness still ruled, with a heavy dose of disbelief.

"Gosh, I hope the game wasn't the last in Brooklyn," Roy Campanella said.

"It's an eerie feeling," Duke Snider said.

Carl Furillo, however, was the realist. "I'm afraid it was the last game in Brooklyn," said the rifle-armed right fielder who saved all those suits for borough president Abe Stark. "It's a sorry bunch to have to leave here. It's a good town."

It was a good town. But it was also the end. The two stars of the final game? Young Danny McDevitt and ageless Gladys Goodding.

Only 6702 fans had paid their way in. The New York *Daily News* hadn't even sent their top name writer. Instead they send a less experienced guy name Chris Kiernan. The last sportswriter to leave Ebbets Field was Dave Anderson, the longtime writer for the New York *Times*, who was with the New York *Journal-American* that evening. He had previously covered the Dodgers for The Brooklyn *Eagle*.

Anderson and Bill Roeder of The New York *World Telegram and Sun* were the last two writers in the press

26

room on the second deck. They rode the little elevator down to the field and walked to the exit near the marble rotunda that served as the main entrance to the park.

"When we approached the night watchman's door, I stepped back to let Bill go first," Anderson recalled many years later in the New York *Times*. "As I followed him out onto Sullivan Place, I realized that I was the last sportswriter to leave Ebbets Field after the last Dodgers game. I didn't mention it to Bill or anyone else. It was just my playful little secret."

The next morning, one had to prowl the sports pages carefully to even find accounts of the game. "Take Them Away, LA! Flock Cops Final, 2-0," said the headline in the New York *Daily News*, the paper with a higher daily circulation than any other in the United States.

Except it wasn't on the back page. Boxing still ruled. The previous night at Madison Square Garden, an iron jawed puncher named Carmen Basilio had defeated Sugar Ray Robinson to win the middleweight title. Everyone was still buzzing about it.

Can you smell rematch?

"Basilio OKs Return Bout!" shouted the headline on the back page. Well, of cour$e he wa$ going to okay it! The Dodgers story was within the paper, adjacent to the boxing. Basilio would later win the Hickok Belt as top professional athlete of the year, something Mantle and Mays had also won.

The Brooklyn Dodgers went to Philadelphia for their final three games of the season. The games were listless as hell. They lost two of them.

During a World Series game between the Yankees and the Milwaukee Braves, the club with Aaron, Spahn, Mathews, no taxes and the big parking lot, a publicist for the Dodgers announced officially that the team would move to Los Angeles in 1958. The publicist read a chilly statement in the press room at the Waldolf Astoria Hotel on

Park Avenue. Walter O'Malley was not there. That day, he was the invisible man. He didn't seem to be anywhere. Sure, just rip the heart out of a vibrant borough and then disappear, why don't you?

After every winter comes a spring, however. So the following spring on April 15, 1958, there was an Opening Day game between the Los Angeles Dodgers and their new old friends the San Francisco Giants at Seals Stadium, where Joe DiMaggio once played in windy San Francisco.

Walter Alston chose Gino Cimoli to be the leadoff batter for the visiting Dodgers. Thus Gino Cimoli, who had scored the final run in the history of Ebbets Field became the first major league batter on the west coast. He struck out against Ruben Gomez.

The Giants won 8-0. The Dodger Giant rivalry was off and running thousands of miles from where it began. It would continue.

Life would go on. But it would never be quite the same.

Your score card should have looked like this.

Chapter 2

Pitching for the New York Giants, Ms. Ida Schnall

The hosts of the Stockholm Olympic Games in 1912 opened the competition to competitive events in swimming and diving to men **and** women. The secretary of the United States Olympic Committee, James E. Sullivan, however, viewed himself as a defender of modesty and did not take kindly to some of the "new modern" swimsuits that many women swimmers were wearing.

The European female athletes had opted for comfortable bathing suits for pool events. Australian swimmer Mina Wylie, who won the 1912 silver medal in the 100 meter freestyle, can be seen here in one of the scandalously comfortable swimsuits that had Mr. Sullivan in such a lather.

Sullivan, a founder of the A.A.U., banned the American

women from competing, huffily citing modesty and
decency. Among those banned was a young woman named
Ida Schnall, one of the finest athletes of her day. She would
make her name in swimming, movies, and - long forgotten
to history - as a pitcher for the New York Female Giants, a
squad of pretty good baseballers who may have been a full
century or more ahead of their time.

Twenty-four year old Ida Schnall never forgot the slight
at the Olympics, nor did she ever give up the challenge of
female athletes finding a fair and level playing field. The
next year, still simmering over her treatment in Stockholm,
she penned a letter to the NY *Times*. The *Times* published
it.

"I read in the newspapers wherein James E. Sullivan is
again objecting to girls competing with the boys in a
swimming contest. He is always objecting, and never doing
anything to help the cause along for a girls' A.A. U. He has
objected to my competing in diving at the Olympic games
in Sweden, because I am a girl," Schnall wrote. "He objects
to girls wearing a comfortable bathing suit. He objects to so
many things that it gives me cause to think that he must be
very narrow minded and that we are in the last century. It's
the athletic girl that takes the front seat today, and no one
can deny it. I only wish that some of our rich sisters would
consider the good they can do with only a small part of
their wealth and start something like an A.A.U. for girls…"

{Author's note: Bravo!}

Over the course of the next few years Ida Schnall won
the women's bicycle race from New York to Philadelphia
and starred on Broadway in Al Jolson's revue, *The Passing
Show of 1912*, where her fancy diving in the harem scene
won her plaudits. She won the grand prize at the San
Francisco Exhibition of 1915 for being "the most
beautifully formed woman in America." Then in 1916 she
went to Hollywood and starred in *Undine*, an American
silent fantasy drama film which featured the athletic actress
Ida Schnall in a water-themed story based upon the French
fairy tale *Undine* by Friedrich de la Motte Fouque, first
published in 1811.

Never mind the plot. As seen here, Schnall played the
Princess and leader of a team of comfortably attired (James
Sullivan would have been horrified!) enchanted water
nymphs. In the film, Schnall dived off a 135-foot cliff in
the Channel Islands off California. No stunt double
necessary, even though her director lied to her about the
height of the cliff. She had been told in advance that the
height was about 80 feet. It was closer to 120.

Then she led her team of aqua-maidens

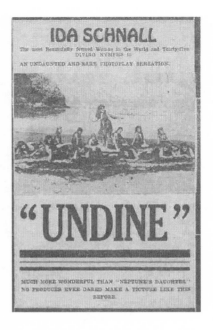

around an enchanted island in a gauzy fantasy. No stunt doubles for this, either.

The film sparked an obscenity trial in Kentucky, which the would-be censors deservedly lost. According to baseball historian John Thorn in his splendid 2012 book, *Baseball in the Garden of Eden: The Secret History of the Early Game,* one critic stated, "No one really cared much about the plot of *Undine*: It was enough that sylphlike Ida Schnall showed up from time to time in various stages of near nudity." Another critic suggested that a better title would have been *Undressed* due to Schnall's wardrobe, or paucity thereof, in the film. Needless to say, the film was a financial success. Sadly, no prints of the entire film are known to remain.

But in 1913, even before going to Hollywood, Schnall and about two dozen other female athletes formed an all-female baseball team named The New York Female Giants and proceeded to play a very brief schedule, including appearances at The Polo Grounds.

The Female Giants comprised 32 players. The women split into two teams, Reds and Blues, and played games against each other. It is likely that the Female Giants were created at least in part by John McGraw. The athletes were mostly high school students.

They were a perhaps a curiosity and seen by many as a mere stunt. But the games were played in earnest and the athleticism legitimate. Ida Schnall, twenty-five years old at the time, was the captain and star player. She also usually pitched. Once at the Polo Grounds, she posed for pictures with Giants' star lefty Rube Marquard, who would later defect to Brooklyn. In regular street clothes, right Schnall hummed a few fastballs for him.

The Female Giants' first game was played on the grounds of the Westchester Golf links on April 27, 1913. More than a thousand fans attended. A game subsequently played on Sunday, May 25, 1913, ended with what can only be described as a police raid. Not only were the ladies violating blue laws, but one of them attempted sell scorecards. The press just happened to be there.

"The batter hitched up her skirt. The pitcher nervously adjusted a side comb," wrote a scribbler for the New York *Tribune*. "Girls will be boys, and the Reds and the Blues of the New York Female Giants were playing an exhibition game at Lenox Oval, 145th Street and Lenox Avenue."

Was this something new? Not exactly. Female athletes had been playing baseball, sort of, at the 'Seven Sisters' colleges of the Northeast since the 1860s. Annie Glidden, a student at Vassar College, was an early player of note. She once wrote a letter home mentioning, "They are getting up various clubs now for out-of-door exercise....They have a floral society, boat clubs and base-ball clubs. I belong to one of the latter, and enjoy it highly, I can assure you."

Here we see Schnall on the mound, pitching.

Good looking, athletic women were no strangers to the Polo Grounds even in the 1890s. Broadway star Helen Dauvray was a fixture at the ancient oval. Recall that she even married a Giant, shortstop John Montgomery Ward. In 1887 La Dauvray funded the first World Series trophy, the "Dauvray Cup," won by the champion Detroit Wolverines.

The first woman to play in Organized Baseball was Lizzie Stride (or Stroud) who on July 5, 1898, with the blessings of the president of the Atlantic League, Ed Barrow, later famous as the general manager of the NY Yankees, tossed an inning for the Reading Coal Heavers against the Allentown Peanuts. (Two hits, no runs.) She later pitched for many years on barnstorming tours. Women also played with professional traveling teams like the "Boston" Bloomer Girls, which was actually based in Kansas City. (Go figure.)

There is no record of the New York Female Giants operating past the 1913 season. They apparently played several games that year and drew more than passing interest from the public. The gates to American female athletes competing in Olympic swimming and diving events opened after 1914 when James Sullivan died.

As years passed, Ida Schnall joined the women's wrestling tour, was a fitness trainer and played tennis on a nearly professional level. Gussy Moran, an American tennis star of the 40s and 50s who played twice in Grand Slam finals, said in 1950 that Ida was, even in her fifties, the greatest woman tennis player who ever lived.

"Maybe she hasn't got the snazziest backhand in the world," Moran noted, "but she tries real hard and cheats like mad. She's great because it's fun to watch her play."

One high profile male whom Schnall offended was Nikola Tesla, the Serbian-American inventor, electrical and mechanical engineer. If the name Tesla sounds familiar, it's because the current day car is named in his honor.

Tesla was dead-set opposed to the "new" woman of the Twentieth Century who wanted to compete with men for jobs, vote and participate in sports. Ida in particular set him off. One time he saw a picture of her boxing with a local welterweight named Willie Bradley who fought at Madison Square Garden in the 1920's.

"In place of the soft voiced, gentle woman of my reverent worship," said Mr. Tesla, "has come the woman who thinks that her chief success in life lies in making herself as much as possible like man in dress, voice and actions, in sports and achievements of every kind."

Ida Schnall, the all-round woman athlete, in a boxing bout with Willie Bradley—a sure indication, according to Mr. Tesla's rather gloomy views, that our civilization is deteriorating

Like many brilliant geeky guys, Tesla was downright weird sometimes, filled with brilliant idea and some loony ideas. There was a 1980 movie on him titled *The Secret Life of Nikola Tesla* which attempts to explain things, complete with Orson Welles (!!!) portraying J. P. Morgan and a lot of funny road-show-Dracula style accents. The production was Yugoslavian and there are some thigh-slapping moments, e.g., although the story is around 1900, give or take a decade or two, all the American flags have fifty stars. America didn't admit its 49th (Alaska) and 50th (Hawaii) states until 1959.

Tesla never married. Poor man! And according to some of the statements he made in the 1920's, babes like Ida Schnall were the reason.

Tesla, by his own explanation, never married young

because his notion of females placed her on such a lofty pedestal that he could never bring himself to feel worthy of her. But then in the 1920's when she skipped down from her pedestal and "bartered all her noblest qualities for what is called her freedom," he was even more set against matrimony than ever. Pressed on the issue, he also explained that chastity was essential to his scientific pursuits.

Famous Scientist Felt Unworthy of Woman as She Used To Be, and Now He Can't Endure Her Trying to Outdo the Men

"I had always thought of woman," said Mr. Tesla, "as possessing those delicate qualities of mind and soul that made her in these respects far superior to man. I had put her on a lofty pedestal, figuratively speaking, and ranked her in certain important attributes considerably higher than man. I worshiped at the feet of the creature I had raised to this height, and, like every true worshiper, I felt myself unworthy of the object of my worship. But all this was in the past. Now the soft-voiced gentle woman of my reverent worship has all but vanished. In her place has come the woman who thinks that her chief success in life lies in making herself as much as possible like man--in dress, voice and actions, in sports and achievements of every kind."

In later years, Schnall moved to Los Angeles, married and stayed there, other than when business or sports put her on the road. She had a love for baseball. She kept forming ball clubs. She reorganized the New York Female Giants in Hollywood in 1928 as well as at least one local team. She died in Los Angeles 1973 at age 85.

Those who knew her, however, always said that the episode in her life of which she was most proud was when she was twenty-five years old and pitched for The New York Female Giants.

*

Bill Wambsganss and his three Dodger Triple play victims, Pete Kilduff, Clarence Mitchell and Otto Miller in 1920.

"When we played the Dodgers in St. Louis,
they had to come through our dugout, and
our bat rack was right there where they
had to walk. My bats kept disappearing,
and I couldn't figure it out. Turns out,
Pee Wee Reese was stealing my bats.
I found that out later, after we got out
of baseball. He and Rube
Walker stole my bats."

Stan Musial

*

"In 1957, I was a sixteen year old

office boy for the Dodgers."

Marv Albert

*

An Ebbets Field Reminiscence

As the oldest grandchild in my family (born in 1941), my Russian born grandfather would do anything for me. I asked him to take me to a ballgame at Ebbets Field. He spoke VERY little English and didn't understand baseball at all.

We had a wonderful evening.

When we got home, my grandmother asked him in Yiddish how he enjoyed the game and his response, of course, was also in Yiddish. My mother was the translator and he said that it was a wonderful evening, but there was one thing he didn't understand.

How in the world could all these people keep yelling "bum" at the ballplayers when they were making $20,000 a year?

There was tremendous rivalry in my house. My father was Giants fan and of course, me a Dodgers fan. I took a ribbing whenever the Giants won and gave it back in spades when the Dodgers won. Of course, it took me an eternity to live down 1951.

I probably had the greatest part time job as a kid. I was an usher in Yankee Stadium and the Polo Grounds. At that age I rooted for two teams, the Dodgers and anyone who played the Yankees. I used to watch the football Giants play and became a huge fan, I was at the championship game in 1956 when we destroyed the Bears. I was at Don Larsen's perfect game in '56. I was also at the famous "greatest game ever played" when the Colts beat the Giants in overtime. Also I was at the Patterson-Johannsen fight at Yankee Stadium in 1959, when Ingemar Johannsen knocked out Floyd Patterson to win the Heavyweight Championship of the World.

Ahhhh, memories. I would have given it all up, if the Dodgers had stayed.

Larry Heyman

Fort Lee, New Jersey

June 2019

Chapter 3

Tex Rickard, Tex Rickards and Tex Rickards

Meet Tex Rickard, Tex Rickards and Tex Rickards.

Both of them. Or all three of them. And then let's put an end to the confusion.

For many years a man named John "Tex" Rickards, was the earthy, gravelly-voiced individual who was the public address announcer at Ebbets Field. Rickards started with the Dodgers in 1924. Before games, he would wander the lower stands and bellow the starting line-ups in a foghorn voice through a large megaphone. When there were line-up changes and pitching changes, he would go through the stands again. The odds were usually about 50-50 that he would get the names right.

A stout amiable man with a resonant voice – to say the least – and an easy self-effacing grin, the fans loved him. Much like superfan Hilda Chester and *Knothole Gang* guy Happy Felton in later years, Rickards was part of the ballpark and part of the Ebbets Field experience. Never mind the mangled names, bloopers and malapropisms. The goofs didn't matter.

"Nobody was angered by his mistakes," Dick Young once wrote in the New York *Daily News*. "They (the Dodger fans) wouldn't have it any other way. He was part of the charm of Ebbets Field. He was a character."

While John Rickards, the announcer, was settling into his job and persona and, dare we say, local celebrity at Ebbets Field, there was also a fellow named George Rickard who was making a big name for himself in the sports world.

George Rickard – no "s" at the end of his name - had been born in Kansas City, Missouri in 1871. He grew up in

45

the Texas towns of Sherman and Henrietta, however, after his family moved to that state when he was a kid. Rickard left school at age nine and became a cowboy at the age eleven. At the age of 23, he was elected marshal of Henrietta, Texas, at which time he began to use the name "Tex."

That same year, 1894, the new sheriff, Tex, decided – for reasons best known to himself - that it might be wise to get out of town pronto. So he departed Texas for Alaska which was still a territory and a rough and tumble place. He discovered gold. He sold his claim, banked his money and ran a hotel in Dawson known as the Northern. He made another fortune, blew it, opened another version of the Northern in Nome and stayed in Alaska for the next twelve years. He travelled to the east coast of the United States a couple of times, then departed for Nevada, following the gold prospectors from one hot site to another.

In Nevada, he started to attend boxing matches on a regular basis. Something about guys beating up on each other appealed to him. Local business leaders wanted to stage a boxing match to publicize their growing community. It didn't matter who would fight. They just wanted a big fight.

Rickard had attended a boxing match in New York, so he got himself hired as the man in charge of making the arrangements. He tried unsuccessfully to sign Terry McGovern and Jimmy Britt, two fighters he had seen in New York at Madison Square Garden back when the Garden was at Madison Avenue and 28th Street.

McGovern - five foot three, 165 pounds - was known as "Terrible Terry," not because he was a bad boxer but because he was a holy terror in the ring. Britt was a one-time Pacific Coast champion, another small man with a huge punch.

The rematch between McGovern and Britt never happened. But Rickard landed Joe Gans and Battling

Nelson, a couple of 'name brawlers,' for $30,000. He staged and promoted a big event on Labor Day, 1906. The receipts were $69,715, the largest ever for a boxing match in the United States. Tex took a healthy chunk off the top for himself.

Although Rickard (seen here in the straw hat) knew little about the sport, he saw the tremendous earning potential of sports promotion. Backed by Montana mining interests, Rickard outbid a legion of others for the right to promote the James J. Jeffries - Jack Johnson fight, a match the simmered with racial tension.

The fight was held in Reno on July 4, 1910. Rickard sold the fight to the public as, "The Fight of the Century," and it certainly was one of them. George "Tex" Rickard was both behind the scenes and on the scene. He sold exclusive film rights for the bout and served as the referee. The film was recorded by nine cameramen and ran two hours long. {Author's note: Like many early fights, it can still be seen on You Tube. That's Tex in the ring as the ref.} Novelist Jack London was also present in the crowd, reporting the event for the Oakland *Tribune*.

Rickard recouped the money paid to the fighters by selling the film rights for $101,000. The fight drew 15,760 fans with a gate of $270,775.

As for the fight itself, reigning champion Jack Johnson, a black American, was in control most of the match. He knocked out former champion Jeffries, a white American, in the fifteenth round of a very one-sided fight. And thereupon the fight assumed even more ugly racial baggage.

The press had dubbed Jeffries "The Great White Hope." White America, much of it, was horrified when Johnson walloped Jeffries. The fight and the film that recorded it caused race riots in many places across the United States. On July 7, 1910, only three days after the fight, various states and cities in the USA declared they would not allow the screening of the footage. The picture was banned across all the states of the Old Confederacy. The fact that Johnson openly consorted with white women didn't help things.

At the urging of Jack Dempsey's manager, Jack (Doc) Kearns, Rickard agreed to promote the Jess Willard-Dempsey championship fight in Toledo, Ohio, in 1919. Although this match was not one of Rickard's most successful promotions, it set the stage for another Dempsey fight, the big one held at Boyle's Thirty Acres near Jersey City on July 2, 1921.

Rickard matched heavyweight champion Dempsey with light heavyweight champion Georges Carpentier. More than 80,000 fans paid a record $1,789,238. Five years later in a Rickard promotion, 120,757 paid $1,895,733 to watch Gene Tunney upset Dempsey. The rematch took place in Soldier Field in Chicago. The slugfest drew 104,943 with a gate of $2,658,660.

Before Rickard came along, fights were chaotic, risky events. Tex brought professionalism and respectability to the business, issuing tickets with prices, dates and seat numbers. He hired security staff who ensured that the buyer got the seat he paid for. When he was the promoter, boxing became respectable, a place a man might take his lady without undue worry so they could both watch guys with no shirts sock each other around the ring. Among the hundreds of fights he promoted was the great Dempsey-Firpo bout of 1923, one of many he promoted at New York's Madison Square Garden.

In short, George (Tex) Rickard led boxing into the era of million-dollar gates and huge crowds. After baseball, boxing was for many decades the second most popular sport in the United States. He developed political clout and was also instrumental in the construction of the third Madison Square Garden. Then he founded the NHL's New York Rangers in 1926 to play in the new building.

On December 26, 1928, Rickard left his home in New York City for Miami Beach, Florida, where he was promoting a fight between Jack Sharkey and "Young" Stribling, a personable heavyweight from Georgia who would later die in a motorcycle accident at age 28.

On New Year's Eve, Rickard was stricken with appendicitis. Doctors operated immediately, but on January 6, 1929 Tex Rickard died due to complications from his appendectomy. His body was placed in a $15,000 bronze casket and lay in the center of Madison Square Garden a few days later. Thousands filed past to pay their respects and get a last glimpse of him.

All of this makes it all the more curious why for many years, many casual observers of the Brooklyn Dodgers thought that Rickard, the deceased boxing promoter, and Rickards, the live-and-in-person Dodgers' public address announcer, were the same guy.

It's not that they looked alike.

They didn't. Here's Tex, the announcer, in a Dodger cap and his trademark sweater, perched beside the Dodger dugout.

And in the mix, as the years went by, there was still a further complication. There was also a Thomas Charles Rickards from Giltbrook, England, an English professional footballer who played as an outside forward.

Rickards played with Notts County, making more than a hundred appearances for the club. He joined Cardiff City in 1938 and followed with one season at that club. World War II brought an end to his professional playing career as he served his country in wartime. After the war, he joined Peterborough United in the Midland Football League, an amateur and semi-pro operation.

Somewhere along the line, Thomas Charles Rickards of Giltbook and John Rickards of Brooklyn started calling themselves "Tex" after the fight promoter. Never mind the missing "s" at the end of their names. Confusion was inevitable.

Back in Brooklyn, a public address system developed in the 1930's. Tex Rickards, the "Dodgers' public address announcer" as he came to be called, was given a chair at the edge of the Dodger dugout. Along with the chair came a brand new microphone and a hook-up to the sound system which could be heard not only all over the ballpark but also along the neighboring streets. Now all those zany goofs and malapropisms were available to a wider and highly appreciative audience.

Addressing Ebbets patrons who had draped their jackets over an outfield wall on a hot day, Rickards once announced, "Will the fans seated along the leftfield railing please remove their clothing?" They removed it, but not in the way one might have imagined.

The request, made many times over the years, was not as idle as one might think. One of the many quirks of Ebbets field was that the left field railing to the field level seats had the final fifteen feet of the white foul line running on top of it. Had a ball landed on an article of clothing draped over the foul line, a ground rule double would have been called, thus affecting play.

Tex, loving his new microphone, could sound like a fan's – or player's – solicitous uncle. One time Preacher Roe left a game in the middle of a solid performance. Rickards grabbed his mike. "The reason Preacher Roe left the game is that he don't feel good," Tex explained.

He would refer to the location of the ticket office as, "the marble rotunda behind me." At the end of a game he would politely ask fans to "not go on the field" but proceed "to the nearest exit to the street," a request that was taken as a cue by a generation or two of Brooklyn kids to run out onto the grass until cleared by security people, many of whom they knew personally.

Tex's daily battle with English language syntax was a marvel. One could only imagine the conversation he might have with crosstown rival, Yogi Berra. Rickards announced one day that a stray child had been "found lost." And at yet another time a lost wallet had been recovered and fans were asked to "form a line" at the lost and found area.

The latter area – the lost and found, wherever that was - was a land mine for complicated explanations. Dick Young also once reported that Tex had announced, "What's ever lost has been found. So, whoever lost it, come up and find it."

Some of this time with the microphone landed Tex in Chateau Bow Wow. He once announced that Ralph Branca had left a game due to a blister, "information" that he'd received from Burt Shotton, the manager. According to Branca, that wasn't the case. During a Dodger pennant race, he announced that Willie Mays had homered in the Giants game. Dodger players were irate that a pro-Giant announcement had been made. "You couldn't print what we thought of that announcement," one Dodger pitcher said.

Rickards countered that Walter O'Malley had asked him to make the announcement, hoping to inspire the Brooks. The players remained unhappy. In 1956, Tex also announced that the next Dodger home game would be played in Jersey City (where the Dodgers played seven games in 1956 as O'Malley played brinksmanship with the city of New York.) Booing ensued for a full minute.

The next season, a game was suspended due to a fog. Chicago Cubs left fielder Bob Speake lost Charley Neal's pop up in the mist. It fell for a double. The umpires suspended play. Tex announced that the game was "being called pending the results of the fog."

Naturally, over the course of three decades and change at Ebbets, Rickards became a popular fixture at the park. Fans knew him. The Dodgers knew him. Visiting press knew him. Opposing players knew him, which brings us to the Bob Rush Story.

In the era in question, the big scoreboard in right field didn't give much information on out of town games. Just the score and the inning. Some of the Dodgers were interested in a St. Louis - Chicago game which affected them. The Cubs were blanking the Cardinals and the Dodger players wanted to know if Bob Rush, who pitched for Chicago from 1948 till 1957, was on the mound. Rush was one of the league's top pitchers, the weak team behind him notwithstanding.

"Hey, Tex!" someone barked from the dugout. "Call the press box and see who's pitching for the Cubs."

Tex grabbed the phone that hung by his chair. He called upstairs to the press box. Someone on the other end said he would check the Western Union ticker tape and call back. A few minutes later Bill Roeder, who covered the Dodgers for The New York *World-Telegram and Sun*, phoned back.

"Hello, Tex?" Roeder said.

"Yes," Tex answered.

"Bob Rush," said Roeder.

A slight pause, then, "Oh, hello, Bob," Rickards said amiably. "How the hell are you?"

Rickards was with the Dodgers for 32 years, through their final game in Brooklyn. But – much like Hilda Chester, Happy Felton, Emmett Kelly and the whole *esprit d'Ebbets* - did not make the move to Los Angeles. Friends said he had not been invited.

He lived at 584 Prospect Avenue for many years and continued to work for his own film delivery business that delivered reels of movies to theaters in Brooklyn. He was 79 years old when he died at the end of October in 1971.

Thirty years later in 2001, one of his personalized metal chairs from Ebbets Field, one which had been beside the Dodger dugout, sold at a memorabilia show for more than $500. Thirteen years later in 2014, one of his distinctive "Dodger announcer" sweaters (as seen in the photo in this chapter) was auctioned off. The winning bid was $1067.

Nearly two grand for Tex's chair and sweater. One wonders what Tex would have said about that. It probably would have been a gem.

The Duke.

Chapter 4

The Greatest Everyday Outfield. Ever!

"A single that goes through to the outfield should score any man from second base," Connie Mack once explained. "But that doesn't go when we play Boston. At Fenway, it takes a double to bring a man home."

What Mr. Mack was referring to, what he saw from the dugout when his powerful Philadelphia A's visited the Boston Red Sox in the early part of the century, was an outfield of Duffy Lewis in left, Tris Speaker in center and Harry Hooper in right, a trio that helped the Red Sox become the best team in baseball in the years leading up to World War I.

There have been many outstanding outfield combinations in the history of baseball. Certain Yankee outfields rate a mention. In the Miller Huggins era, Bob Meusel, Earle Combs and Babe Ruth won three pennants together. Joe McCarthy fielded the impressive trio of Charlie Keller, Joe DiMaggio and Tommy Henrich that played on several pennant winners in the World War II era.

But there are compelling arguments why the trio of Lewis, Speaker and Hooper should be ranked as the greatest outfield ever to play day-in day-out for one team over an extended period of time.

First off, they all could hit. Hooper averaged .281 over 17 seasons. Lewis batted .284 over 11 campaigns, and with power. Speaker's .344 over 22 years speaks for itself. But it was in the outfield that they redefined the defensive alignments of baseball. All three had speed and were blessed with superior arms. They threw out so many base runners trying to take an extra base or score that coaches routinely held back men who could easily have advanced. Mr. Mack's words were no exaggeration: From 1910 through 1915, the years the greatest of all outfields played together on the Red Sox, an opposing team often needed a double to safely bring home a man from second.

Speaker was the finest of the three. Only a Mays, Mantle or DiMaggio was comparable in the field. Sportswriters called Speaker, "the fifth infielder." Batters and base runners could have explained why.

Speaker liked to lurk behind second base, where he could stare a batter in the eye. Little bloops and flares over second and short were easy outs for the Gray Eagle. When a ball was hit over his head, he retreated like a rocket and routinely pulled the ball in with a graceful over-the-shoulder catch.

Speaker played from 1907 to 1928, and thus his career spanned the dead and lively ball eras. On today's artificial surfaces he would be forced to position himself in deeper center. But even when the lively ball was introduced, he compensated only gradually. Few batters could drive anything over his head.

Speaker concocted a pair of dazzling set plays involving second base. In one, he would hesitate on a short line drive in his direction, appearing to lose the ball—or to be planning to take it on a bounce. The runner would take off toward third. Then the Gray Eagle would soar in at full speed, catch the ball on the run and continue to second base. Unassisted double play. John McGraw's unsuspecting Giants were victimized on that play in the seventh game of the 1912 World Series.

Speaker's other favorite involved no fewer than five Red Sox fielders. He teamed most effectively with his best friend on the team, pitcher Joe Wood. With a runner on second, Wood and his catcher would stall, as if confused over signs. The shortstop and second baseman would distract the runner yet remain far from the bag. Speaker would charge in from short center, whereupon Wood would turn and throw. The astonished runner would find Tris waiting there to tag him out. Just your routine 1-8 pickoff, if you're scoring.

In right field, Harry Hooper was almost Speaker's equal defensively. No one was better at shoestringing a short line drive off the top of the grass—he virtually patented the rump-slide catch. Similarly, Hooper was unparalleled at racing back to the short wall in right field and pulling balls away from the outstretched fingers of Boston spectators. A long-forgotten catch Hooper made against the Giants in the fifth inning of the final game of the 1912 Series must rank as the equal of the 1954 Willie Mays catch against Vic Wertz, the 1955 Sandy Amoros catch against Yogi Berra or the 1947 catch against DiMaggio by Al Gionfriddo. Put Ron Swoboda (1969) and Joe Rudi (1972) into the discussion, also.

Hooper went all the way to the wall chasing a fly hit by Giants second baseman Larry Doyle. But he didn't stop at the wall—he tumbled over it, catching the ball while falling completely out of the playing field. More astounding was that he made the catch with his bare hand. It prevented the Giants from scoring enough runs to win the game in nine innings. In the 10th the Giants aided a Red Sox rally by letting an easy foul pop by Speaker drop among three fielders. Given another life, Speaker singled home the tying run before Larry Gardner wrapped up the Series for the Sox with a sacrifice fly.

In leftfield, Duffy Lewis didn't have the raw speed of Hooper and Speaker, but he had uncanny baseball intuition. Slightly chunkier than his teammates, he also had the Wall – it was painted black back then, not green - behind him and Speaker next to him. So he compensated by playing much closer to the foul line than other fielders of his era, allowing Speaker to streak into left center and poach. But in tribute to Lewis's own prowess, the raised area at the base of the leftfield wall in Fenway was known for years as Duffy's Cliff.

Lewis also was a hitter with surprising power. He was often among the American League home run or RBI leaders. A righthanded hitter, he might have hit 35 homers a year in Fenway with today's supercharged baseball. One of his most notable victims was Grover Cleveland Alexander, whom Lewis personally devastated with a five for eight performance in Boston's 1915 World Series victory over Philadelphia.

"That guy hits me as if I were a bush leaguer," Alexander moaned afterward.

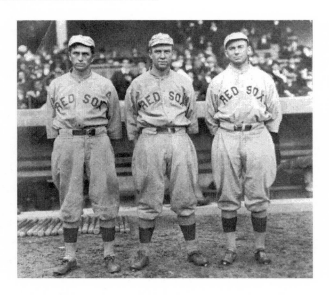

Lewis, Speaker and Hooper arrived in Boston around the same time. Speaker came first, in 1907. When he failed to impress Red Sox management, he was dealt to the Little Rock minor league club, supposedly as compensation for the use of their spring training camp. Later, after destroying the Southern Association with a .350 batting average, Speaker was returned to the Hub for $400.

Hooper and Lewis both came to the Red Sox by way of St. Mary's College in California and the California

State League. Hooper arrived in 1909, Lewis a year later. Unlike Speaker, they became regulars the moment they joined the Sox. With the opening of Fenway Park in 1912, everything jelled at once, and Boston became the powerhouse of the American League. In an era when a good outfielder might average a dozen assists a year, the Boston trio several times had upwards of 80 among them. Speaker twice had an American League-record 35 by himself even though runners and coaches quickly learned to take few liberties on the base paths.

The end of this era began with something not unusual in Red Sox history—a contract squabble between management and a star player. During the bidding war with the rival Federal League in 1914-15, Speaker's salary was increased from $9,000 to $18,000. With the demise of the upstart league after Boston had won the 1915 World Series, Red Sox owner Joe Lannin celebrated by trying to cut the Gray Eagle back to $9,000.

Speaker held out, long and bitterly. The dispute that followed ended on Opening Day 1916 when Speaker was peddled to the Cleveland Indians. Boston repeated as world champions that year—Lewis and Hooper were joined in the outfield by Tilly Walker—but seeds of discontent had been sown.

Lannin sold the franchise to Harry Frazee, the Broadway producer who would eventually find fame producing *No, No, Nanette!* Someone ought to have said, "No, No!" to Harry, or maybe a more emphatic, "Hell, no, Harry! 'Sa matter with you, you schmuck? Don't do it!"

Frazee's favorite method of raising cash was to sell Red Sox stars, particularly to the Yankees. As is well known to sports fans from New Jersey to Boston's North End, his most egregious move was dealing Babe Ruth south in 1920.

Duffy Lewis went into the Navy during World War I and missed the entire 1918 season. When he returned to baseball in 1919, he was a Yank, along with Ernie Shore and Dutch Leonard, soon to be joined by Carl Mays, Waite Hoyt and Herb Pennock. Somehow, Harry Hooper missed the train to Grand Central and went to the White Sox instead.

   The Red Sox hit the second division as soon as Hooper departed in 1921. They dropped to the league basement in 1922. There the Bosox wallowed until 1934, finishing seventh once and eighth eight times over the next 12 years. Some historians maintain that the club never fully recovered until the double play combo of Theo Epstein and Terry Francona came along early in the next century.

   In the decades that followed, the great outfield of the Red Sox glory years was reunited occasionally at Old-Timers' events. (L-> R Lewis, Speaker and Hooper) Speaker passed away first, at the age of 70, in 1958. Hooper left professional baseball and served as a postmaster in California for many years before his death in 1974 at 87. Duffy Lewis, a durable baseball man, served as road secretary for the Milwaukee Braves until well into his '70s. When he died in 1979, he was 91.

Here is a footnote to the careers of Lewis, Speaker and Hooper, a reflection of their excellence: None of them ever played for a loser in the World Series. Hooper was the right fielder on four Red Sox winners—1912, 1915, 1916 and 1918. Lewis was the leftfielder on the first three. Speaker was in center for the first two championships before being shipped to Cleveland. There he resurfaced as the player-manager for the Indians' 1920 World Series victory over Brooklyn, managed by Uncle Robbie.

By that time, of course, the Boston franchise was in its long decline. And the new powers of the league, the Indians and Yankees, were stocked with the elements of perhaps the greatest outfield ever.

But if you like footnotes as much as the author of this book, you'll probably enjoy this one, too. Any article on Red Sox outfielders would be remiss without mention of Ted Williams and Carl Yastrzemski, the two men who roamed the pasture in front of the wall after it was painted green in the 1940's.

This all ties together with another Red Sox outfielder named Carol Hardy.

On September 20, 1960 season, Ted Williams was in the final days of his Hall of Fame career before an often unappreciative Boston audience. Ted fouled a ball off his foot in the first inning of a game against the Orioles in Baltimore. Carol Hardy was on the bench for the Boston Red Sox. After Ted limped off the field, Hardy finished the at bat for him, becoming the only player ever to pinch hit for The Thumper. {The Orioles won 4-3; another Hall of Famer, Hoyt Wilhelm earned the save.}

Hardy quickly lined into a double play.

Eight days later at Fenway Park, in his final major league appearance, Williams hit his 521st and last home run against Jack Fisher of the Baltimore Orioles. In the ninth inning, he was replaced by Hardy in left field.

"They booed me all the way out and cheered him all the way in," Hardy recalled many times over the years.

Then, early the next season, May 31, 1961, Hardy pinch-hit for rookie Carl Yastrzemski, making him the only player in major league history to go in for both future Hall of Famers. Hardy pinch hit three times that year for Yaz. He doubled twice. "Yaz was a rookie, and early on he had trouble with lefties,'' says Hardy. "But he figured it out.''

On Dec. 10, 1962, he was traded to the Colt .45s for Dick Williams, who would eventually manage the 1967 "Impossible Dream'' Red Sox. Oddly, Hardy was on the bench for the Twins when Yaz and the BoSox won the pennant.

But here's how it all comes back to the greatest outfield ever.

Early in his career, Hardy played for the Cleveland Indians (where he once also pinch hit for Roger Maris.) In Cleveland, one of his batting coaches was Tris Speaker, rounding out another episode in the endlessly perfect geometry of baseball.

*

"I rooted for the Dodgers when they were in Brooklyn."

Kareem Abdul-Jabbar

Ebbets Field Reminiscence

My father, Alan Hynd, was a true crime writer from 1920 until the 1960s. His specialties were murders and swindles. Since he worked for newspapers and magazines in Boston, New Jersey, Philadelphia and New York he had no shortage of jaw-dropping material. From time to time I met some of the people he wrote about. Not so much the victims, but the perps. It was, to say the least, an education. And yes, this is about The Dodgers and Ebbets Field.

The one partial break he took from crime was to write stories that supported the war effort in first half of the 1940's. He authored two books that became national best sellers in 1943, *Passport To Treason* and *Betrayal From the East*. During this time, he also wrote for some of the best magazines of the day. For a guy who never finished high school, it was impressive stuff.

From time to time he did profiles on the men who fought the war. One such was Lt. General Clare Lee Chennault. Lt. General Chennault was a colorful seat-of-the-pants character who commanded The First American Volunteer Group (AVG) of the Chinese Air Force in 1941–1942. The AVG was nicknamed the Flying Tigers. It was composed of fighter pilots from the United States Army Air Corps, the U.S. Navy, and U.S. Marine Corps. The aircraft were to fly with Chinese colors but be under American

control. The mission was to bomb Japan and defend China, which they did with Curtiss P-40 Warhawks bedecked with smiling shark teeth, one of the most iconic images of the war. The P-40 was an American single engine single seat, all-metal fighter and ground-attack aircraft, a devasting machine. The Tigers flew the P-40's in combat after the US and Japan declared war and were the first group to bomb Japan, an astonishing twelve days after Pearl Harbor. Their successes were astounding. The Flying Tigers destroyed 296 Japanese aircraft, while losing only fourteen pilots in combat. They were not just national heroes, but they were world famous.

Sometime in 1943 or 1944, General Chennault and some of his warriors were in New York to help sell war bonds and confer with my father on a prominent magazine story. After the article was wrapped up, there was some time left, a few days I think. My father asked what the guys would like to do in New York before they returned to the merciless combat in the South Pacific. Name the impossible and he'd see if he could arrange it.

The airmen, there were six of them including the commander, huddled and whispered to each other. Everyone nodded. They seemed to agree on something. One of them announced their wish. "We'd like to go to Ebbets Field," he said. "We'd like to see the Dodgers."

As it happened, there was a major pennant race and the top team in the National League, the St. Louis Cardinals, was in town. The best seats, maybe all the seats, were gone. You didn't put guys like this in the bleachers, you just didn't do it, even though they would have easily accepted.

"The ticket office won't have anything," my father said. "Let me phone the front office and see what I can do."

The call was made. My father identified himself. He was writing, I think, for *The American Mercury* at the time. He said his guests were important people. The request was met with skepticism. There was nothing available. Go away. My father, having a couple of decades experience as a nosy reporter, knew he should keep the conversation going until the guy on the other end asked the question my father was waiting for.

"Who are your guests who are so damned important?" asked the Dodger rep.

That was exactly the question my father, a skilled questioner, wanted. Time to pounce.

"Lt. General Clare Chennault and five of the Flying Tigers," he said. "I'm sure you've heard of them."

A heavy pause, then, "Hold on. Just a minute."

The call went up the chain of command faster than one of those Warhawks taking off. Another voice came on the line. Eight box seat tickets were suddenly available behind the Dodger dugout. The tickets would be available in the marble rotunda and we all know where that was.

Some people from the front office would come out to make sure everything went smoothly.

The six airmen went in uniform. The crowd applauded them as they entered. My father got the seventh seat. My mother got the eighth.

I once asked my father who won the game.

Without missing a beat he answered, "We all did."

Noel Hynd
Los Angeles
May 2019

{Author's note: *Ashes From a Burning Corpse* is a novelized account of Alan Hynd's involvement in a high profile murder case in the Bahamas in 1943.}

*

"Not getting booed at Ebbets Field was an amazing thing. Those fans knew their baseball and Gil {Hodges} was the only player I can remember whom the fans never, I mean never booed."

Clem Labine

*

"If you had a son, it would be a great thing to have him grow up to be just like Gil Hodges."

Pee Wee Reese

*

"Gil Hodges is a Hall of Fame man."

Roy Campanella

Chapter 5 - Robinson and Ruth

No, sorry. This is not about Jackie Robinson or Babe Ruth.

The question is sometimes asked as to exactly when the Giants-Dodgers rivalry began.

Both the Brooklyn and the New York clubs fielded competitive teams in the National League of the 1890's. The seeds of the modern rivalry did begin there. The dominant team in baseball in that era was the Baltimore Orioles, led by fiery John McGraw, the third baseman and sparkplug and his friend, Oriole catcher Wilbert Robinson. Robinson was a fine hitter and fine handler of pitchers and a great catcher. He was also an iron man. He once caught a triple header for the Orioles in the 1890's, then caught a doubleheader the next day.

When McGraw came to New York in 1902 and became the player-manager of the New York Giants, he brought Robinson along as his pitching coach. Robinson was coach and mentor to Christy Mathewson, Rube Marquard, Iron Man McGinnity and the other great Giant hurlers of the first decade of the Twentieth Century. As manager and coach, best buddies and business partners, Robinson and McGraw never seemed to be more than a short pop fly away from each other.

Eventually, a feud developed between them. McGraw claimed that Robinson had missed a key sign as a coach in the 1913 World Series which the Giants lost to the Philadelphia A's. The following year, Charlie Ebbets, President of the Dodgers, hired Robinson to come over Brooklyn to be his manager. Robinson agreed. Ebbets had grand plans to resuscitate a struggling franchise in an outer borough of New York City. A new field with his name on it was part of the plan. A new manager was another part.

The great sportswriter John Kiernan of The New York *Times* wrote of Robinson, "It is doubtful that baseball ever produced a more colorful figure… Like Falstaff, he was not only witty himself but the cause of wit in others. His conversation was a continuous flow of homely philosophy, baseball lore, and good humor." Another contemporary writer extolled Robinson's "affable serenity" and another affectionately referred to him as, "a pleasantly profane fat man."

In August of 1908 a pair of wealthy Washington Senators fans, Preston Gibson and John Biddle, had obviously passed too much time in the Devil's workshop. They made a wager with each other as to whether a baseball tossed from the top of the Washington Monument could be caught. No one knew because no one had ever been nutsy enough to try it. The ball would free fall 555 feet and accelerate. Who wanted any part of that?

The two men enticed Washington's splendid defensive catcher Gabby Street to be the guinea pig. Street, a tough character who never minced away from a challenge, rose to the moment. He showed up at the monument on a summer morning before a game against Ty Cobb and the Detroit Tigers.

The betting men climbed to the summit of the monument with a basket full of baseballs. They brought with them a wooden chute so the ball would slide many feet from the structure and clear the wide base of the monument.

The first 10 baseballs failed to clear the base. So the two fans junked the chute and took turns throwing the balls from their site in the sky.

Street, dressed in street clothes, no pun intended, stood below with his arms outstretched over his head as if to corral a pop fly. He could barely see the balls when they left the top of the monument. But Street made a successful catch on the fifteenth attempt, and not without some drama.

"I didn't see the ball until it was halfway down," said Gabby. "It was slanting in the wind and I knew it would be a hard catch."

The baseball had accelerated to almost 100 miles an hour as it plunged and had picked up 300 pounds of force by the time it landed in Street's mitt. The mitt almost hit the ground from the impact, Street's hands along with it.

But catch it he did. He then dusted himself off and continued on his way to Boundary Field, where the Senators played their home games and where the Howard University Hospital now stands. He caught nine innings of Walter Johnson that afternoon. The Senators topped the Detroit Tigers on a five-hitter, 3-1, none of the hits off the bat of the ever-cheerful Ty Cobb, who was oh-for-four.

All of the above brings us to Uncle Robbie, the second year Brooklyn manager in 1915 and an employee of Charlie Ebbets who loved quirky publicity. Uncle Robbie, an ex-catcher don't forget, had always pooh-poohed Street's catch as having not been so difficult. So, upping the ante, Ebbets asked if any of Robinson's players would attempt to catch the opening pitch of the season at Ebbets Field that year. No big deal, but the "pitch" was to be a baseball dropped from an airplane in the sky.

No player was crazy enough to volunteer.

Robinson by this time was 53 years old, slow and pudgy. He had not caught a major league game since 1902. Ebbets asked if Robbie might catch the baseball from the airplane.

Crazy? Sure. But, "I'll give it a try," said Robinson at spring training at Daytona Beach, Florida.

Robbie did, however, want to practice.

In the area that spring was a young pilot named Ruth Law, also known by her married name, Ruth Law Oliver. A photogenic lady of twenty-eight, Law was one of America's great early aviatrixes. Harry Atwood and Arch Freeman at Atwood Park in Massachusetts taught her to fly, after Orville Wright of Kitty Hawk fame in 1903 had refused.

A controlled aircraft in the sky remained a stunning sight for most people. Even more stunning was flying one of those machines, and more incredible was a female pilot. The ladies couldn't even vote yet. But Ruth Law had received her pilot's license in November 1912. What was the point of having such a license and not going up there among the clouds?

Ruth also had a personal ax to grind. She had been refused aeronautics lessons by Orville Wright because, according to Law, Orville held to the quaint notion that women didn't understand mechanics. The snub only made her more determined. "The surest way to make me do a thing is to tell me I can't do it," she later said. Not surprisingly, Ruth's brother, Rodman Law, was an aviator and stunt man in silent movies, specializing in parachute

drops. From time to time, he was known as "The Human Fly." (Here they are together in Ruth's aircraft.) On February 2, 1912 Rodman Law - presumably with nothing more exciting to do - parachuted off the top of the candle of the Statue of Liberty then later starred in several short stunt man films, including one that was shot on the Williamsburg Bridge. No copies of his silent movies have survived.

It wasn't surprising to find Ruth Law buzzing through the skies above Daytona Beach in 1915 giving a demonstration of aerobatics before a large astonished crowd. She announced ahead of time that she was going to perform a loop for the first time. She proceeded to do exactly that, not once but twice, to the heart-stopping amazement of her husband, Charles Oliver.

Among those who knew of Ruth Law was Wilbert Robinson. Why not, someone suggested, have a practice run at catching a baseball dropped from an aircraft by a celerity aviatrix? Robinson who frequently wandered amiably into borderline-insane events like this, said he would have a go at it.

The day arrived during Brooklyn spring training. So did the intrepid Ruth Law in her biplane.

Out of the plane at the appointed hour came a small round object that at first was a dark speck in the sky. Then as it fell it grew both brighter and larger until, with the porky Uncle Robbie circling under it, it came closer and closer and...

Splat!

"It caromed off the edge of his mitt and hit him right in the chest," Casey Stengel, the Brooklyn right fielder, a witness, later recalled. It figured that Casey would be at such an event. "It spun him around. Then he fell over, like in a Western picture where you see an Indian that's out on the hill, and they shoot him, and he goes around in a circle and falls dead."

Concerned, the Brooklyn players raced to Robinson's side, where they found him covered with a sticky reddish-yellowish gooey mess, the remains of a pink grapefruit that had been substituted for a baseball. Robinson thought he had lost an eye or been mortally wounded, seeing the reddish remains of the fruit.

Then he took it in stride.

Ruth Law explained later that part of her flight that morning was dropping golf balls onto a local golf course. When she arrived over the baseball field, she couldn't find the baseball. So she substituted the fruit. That was her story and she stuck to it.

The plans for the Opening Day ball drop were scuttled. But Uncle Robbie had plenty more to laugh about as the season progressed. For one thing, his "Robins" (as the Brooklyn team was now called in his honor) were steadily rising in the standings. Better yet, toward the end of the season the Giants plopped into last place. There they stayed, the great Connie Mack and the great John McGraw occupying the basement at the same time. The Dodgers finished third.

But let's get back to Ruth Law for a moment, who was having a better mid-decade.

In the spring of 1916, she took part in an altitude competition, twice narrowly coming in second to male fliers. She was furious, determined to set a record that would stand against men as well as women. Eventually, she set a new cross-country distance record by flying from Chicago, Illinois, to Hornell, New York, in a Curtiss Pusher biplane similar to the one seen here were her name on it.

After the United States entered World War One in April 1917, she campaigned unsuccessfully for women, including herself, to be allowed to fly military aircraft. The top brass wouldn't allow it. Stung by her rejection, she wrote a feisty opinion piece entitled *Let Women Fly!* in a new magazine, *Air Travel*. She argued that success in aviation should prove a woman's fitness for work in that field. Ruth Law then underscored her point by earning as much as $9,000 a week for exhibition flights in 1917.

Many patriotic American women volunteered to fly and fight for their country in World War One, including Ruth Law. None was accepted by the military. Many American women pilots volunteered. None were taken seriously.

After the great war, Law continued to set records and participate in aircraft exhibitions.

At Toronto, Ontario, Saturday, June 29, 1918, she flew an airplane in a race against a Chevrolet. The car was actually Ford. But the driver was a handsome cocky young man named Gaston Chevrolet, of the French-Swiss family that founded the American auto manufacturer. The race was to cover 5 laps. Chevrolet was given a one-lap head start and won the race by half a lap with Ruth noisily gaining on him overhead. Smoke billowed from both vehicles and they hit the finish line seconds apart. She was gaining when the race ended. Had there been another lap, she probably would have won.

After Raymonde de Laroche of France set a women's altitude record of nearly 13,000 feet on June 7,

1919, Law set a new French woman's record on June 10, flying to 14,700 feet. Laroche in turn, however, broke Oliver's record on 12 June, flying to a height of 15,748 feet.

Ruth Law's greatest feat took place on November 19, 1916. She broke the existing cross-America flight air speed record of 452 miles by flying nonstop from Chicago to New York State, a distance of 590 miles. The next day she flew on to New York. Flying over Manhattan, her fuel ran out, but she glided to a safe landing on Governors Island. President Woodrow Wilson attended a dinner held in her honor on 2 December 1916.

In 1917, she was the first woman authorized to wear an American military uniform, but she was denied permission to fly in combat. Instead, she raised money for the Red Cross and Liberty Loan drives with exhibition flights.

"There is a world-old controversy that crops up whenever women attempt to enter a new field. Is a woman fit for that work?" Ruth Law wrote at the time. "It would seem that a woman's success in any particular field would prove her fitness for that work, without regard to theories to the contrary."

When the war ended, she formed "Ruth Law's Flying Circus," a zippy three-plane troupe that dazzled spectators at state and county fairs across the United States. They raced against cars, flew through fireworks, and established new altitude and distance records.

The thrills and honors were short-lived, however. One morning in 1922, she opened the newspaper to read a report that she had retired. Her husband, Charles Oliver, could no longer bear his wife's hazardous occupation and had ordered an end to her flying career. He had mailed out the notices himself.

These days, she might have dumped the crusty old goat. A century ago, however, a woman deferred to her husband, however unreasonable. She turned to gardening.

In 1932, she had a nervous breakdown that she attributed to lack of flying.

During World War Two, however, Ruth Law's ideas finally found receptive ears. Women were admitted to an auxiliary corps. Among them was Women Airforce Service Pilots (WASP) which trained and ferried military planes from base to base within the United States. Between September 1942 and December 1944, the WASPs delivered 12,650 aircraft of 78 different types. Each woman who flew freed a male pilot for combat missions, a dubious honor.

Thirty-eight WASP fliers lost their lives in accidents while serving. Eleven died during training. Twenty-seven perished on active duty. Because they were not officially part of the military, under the existing guidelines, a fallen WASP was sent home at family expense. Traditional military honors or notes of heroism, such as medals, permission to allow the U.S. flag to be placed on the coffin or displaying a service flag in a window, were not allowed.

Nonetheless, Ruth Law saw many of her early ideas become reality. She died in San Francisco in December of 1970 at the age of eighty-three, sixty-five years after the day she dropped the famous grapefruit on the unsuspecting Uncle Robbie.

Gabby Street, the old catcher and later manager whose attempts to catch the ball off Washington Monument led to Uncle Robbie being splattered by the foxy aviatrix's grapefruit, did well for himself.

Almost three decades later, Street returned to St. Louis where he had been a successful player and manager with the Cardinals (Pennants in 1928 and 1930 and 1931) and as unsuccessful as everyone else with the Browns in 1938. He was now a broadcaster. As a color commentator on the St. Louis Browns radio broadcasts after World War Two, he worked with a younger microphone partner who had been born in St. Louis with the name of Harry Christopher Carabina.

As a younger man serving time in Joliet, Illinois, the town not the prison, Carabina had been advised by WCLS station manager Bob Holt to change his name to something less awkward on the air. Thus - Holy cow! - Harry Carabina became Harry Caray, seen here with a microphone, and began a Hall of Fame career up and down the American Midwest as one of the most popular baseball broadcasters of all time.

All in all, he did far better than Gaston Chevrolet who had beaten Ruth Law around that oval in Ontario. After his May 31, 1920 victory at the Indianapolis 500, Chevrolet moved on to California to the compete on the Beverly Hills Speedway, a 1.25-mile wooden board track. That track was built for early auto racing on a parcel of land that today includes The Beverly Wilshire Hotel. Chevrolet (seen here with the moustache and the strange *Je*

79

m'en fous expression) died when his Frontenac crashed on lap 146 of the 200-lap race. He was 28 years old.

Sadly, Ruth Law's older brother, Rodman, died young, also. Law had suffered a serious injury while performing a stunt in 1914. During the long hospitalization, most of the money he had made in films had dissipated in hospital bills.

Law had almost given up stunt work, but when the US entered World War I, Law, a patriot, enlisted in the Army Aviation Corps. He was assigned to Kelly Field in Texas where he taught parachute jumping. There he contracted tuberculosis. He died of the disease at Camp Sevier in Greenville, South Carolina on October 14, 1919, after being hospitalized for a few months.

As for Uncle Robbie, he became the symbol of the Brooklyn club for a generation, managing the team into their first pennants in 1916 and 1920 and their first respectability in the modern era. Thereafter, the team descended into the "Daffy Dodger" comedies of the mid to late 1920's. Midway into his tenure as the Brooklyn manager, he discarded the uniform and wore street clothes to manage. He was part of the tableau at Ebbets Field, often in a straw hat at the edge of the dugout, gesturing to or encouraging his players. We see him here with Brooklyn Dodgers stars of the 1920's, Jack Fournier and Zack Wheat.

Robinson and John McGraw made peace at the National League winter meetings in December 1930, ending their long estrangement. Robinson remained on as Brooklyn manager through the end of the 1931 season, after which he left for a hunting trip in Georgia.

He wasn't there long when he received word that the Dodgers had replaced him as manager with Max Carey. Fired, in other words. In 1932 Robinson became president and manager of the Atlanta Crackers of the Southern Association. In the late summer 1934, still chugging amiably along at age 71, he fell in his hotel room, hitting his head on the bathtub and breaking his arm.

"Don't worry about it, fellas," he said to the doctors who came to his assistance. "I'm an old Oriole. I'm too tough to die."

Sadly, he had suffered a cerebral hemorrhage from the fall. He died a few days later with his wife of many years at his bedside. It was less than six months after the passing of McGraw. The two old Oriole teammates are buried at New Cathedral Cemetery in Baltimore just a short pop fly away from each other.

*

**"Brooklyn was a famous team.
I wanted to play for the Dodgers."**

Roberto Clemente

An Ebbets Field Reminiscence

A HERO RETURNS

I don't remember what induced me to become a Brooklyn Dodger fan, although the year I declared "all-in" coincides with the year of Mickey Owen's infamous passed ball (1941) and the awful events that immediately followed. I had just reached the rebellious age of nine when underdogs were enormously appealing, even though being a Dodger fan in the early '40s in Scarsdale, New York, was a lonely road to follow.

Except for a sprinkling of Giant fans, the majority of my schoolmates backed the Yankees with smug confidence. Their heroes back then were Spud Chandler, Bill Bevens, Frankie Crosetti, and Snuffy Stirnweiss. Mine were Dolph Camilli, Augie Galan, Luis Olmo, and Frenchy Bordagaray. But then came the post-war resurgence of major league talent, and the coming to the Dodgers of Robinson, Snider, Hodges, Reese, and Campanella.

But the Yankee ranks grew in talent as well, and at the height of the Dodger-Yankee rivalry, the agony of defeat became a frequently experienced occurrence. Revenge was realized when, as an Army private in Munich, Germany in 1955, the Armed Forces Radio Service brought news of Johnny Podres' victory over the Yankees in the final game of the 1955 World Series.

It would be a short celebration.

Two years later, the glitter of Los Angeles gold beckoned. For an *auslander* like me, disavowing allegiance to Dem Bums was about as easy as turning off a light switch. It would be a far different matter for the

83

homegrown Brooklyn fan as I was to learn thirty years later when Duke Snider came back to town.

I chose book publishing for a career in the early '60s, and in 1987, as a senior editor at Zebra Books, I learned that my boss, Walter Zacharius, who owned the company and, not so incidentally, was born and bred in Brooklyn, had bought book rights to Duke Snider's autobiography. I was assigned to overseeing the manuscript through to its print stage.

Titled *The Duke of Flat*bush, it was ably co-authored by Bill Gilbert, and released the following summer on Father's Day. A noon signing was scheduled at Barnes and Noble's flagship Fifth Avenue store.

Sunday, June 19, 1988, dawned sunny and hot. It was the kind of Manhattan heat that made you feel you were leaving footprints in the asphalt whenever you crossed the street. Standing outside for any length of time was a matter for the foolhardy. I picked up Snider at the Downtown Athletic Club and drove uptown before turning left on 45th Street. It was well before noon when we approached Fifth Avenue and saw a long line of people that started at Barnes and Noble's front door and continued north to 46th Street where it turned the corner and moved westward toward Sixth Avenue.

"Are all those folks here to see me?" Snider wondered aloud. Later in the day the store's manager told me it was the biggest signing they'd ever had.

Once inside the store, Snider settled into a chair behind the signing desk and the organized onslaught began. It seemed that practically every customer who approached the desk with Duke's book in one hand also brought an article of memorabilia from the days before Ebbets Field became Ebbets Field Apartments in the other. A cornucopia of old Dodger programs, scorecards, bubblegum baseball cards, yellowing baseballs, and snapshots of Snider taken from the centerfield grandstands, saw sunlight for the first time in decades.

Each and every book and piece of memorabilia was signed with a warm smile and a handshake from the man who had remained a hero to so many. Snider left for a one o'clock TV interview, and shortly afterwards a young woman in tears ran into the store shouting, "Is he still here? He hasn't left, has he?"

It seemed she and her father had not spoken for quite a number of years and she hoped that a Father's Day gift of a book written and signed by her father's hero would open the door to reconciliation. She received a signed copy of the *Duke of Flatbush*, and I can only hope it did the trick.

It is said that, back in the day, you could walk down any street in Brooklyn in the summertime, and, if it was warm enough for apartment windows to be opened, you could follow the progress of the game from block to block through the radio voice of Red Barber. With that Father's Day in 1988, I came to understand the genuine pain the long-suffering homegrown fans felt when their beloved team pulled up roots and departed for the distant West Coast.

It would have been far more than the Kid from Scarsdale could ever have imagined.

Wallace Exman

Osterville, MA

June 2019

Gil, Campy and the Duke of Flatbush

*

"That was a tough break for Mickey to get. I bet he feels like a nickel's worth of dog meat."

**Tommy Henrich, on
Mickey Owen's passed ball.**

*

"Being Captain of the Dodgers meant representing an organization committed to winning and trying to keep it going. We could have won every year if the breaks had gone right."

Pee Wee Reese

Chapter 6

The 1923 World Series – All Power To The Bronx

In 1912 the New York baseball club in the American League was a sorry operation. Known as the Highlanders, they played in rickety, wooden Hilltop Park at Broadway and 165th Street and finished last in the American League.

A few blocks away, John J. McGraw's New York Giants were the most famous team in baseball—the most feared, the most loved, the most envied, the most imitated. They were also the incarnation of McGraw's vision of the game: "Inside baseball," he called it, "scientific baseball," a shrewd amalgam of bunts, steals, sacrifices, platoons and strategies, which also included clever ways to cheat or intimidate opponents. Play for a run or two, then make them stand up. This was the old-style game—refined and purified, to be sure—played the way it had been since Grandpa's time. But McGraw had elevated it to an art form. The Giants became the team to beat every year, not just in New York, but anywhere.

Thus, it was seen as almost an act of charity when, in 1913, the Giants invited the Highlanders to move into the Polo Grounds as tenants. The Highlanders—they changed their name to the Yankees later that year—were threats to no one but themselves. The Giants were simply letting their little brothers use the equipment when the real ball club was away.

But in 1915 the Yankees were acquired by an aggressive new ownership – getting rid of some notorious Tammany Hall types in the process. Over the next few years they began playing a new kind of game, going for power throughout the lineup. They aimed for the big inning, runs in clusters, and as a result they moved toward the top of the American League standings. In his biography, *Babe,* Robert W. Creamer compared the 1919 Yankees to John the Baptist preparing the way for the Lord.

Well, Holy Short Porch in Right Field!

The Lord, of course, was Babe Ruth. In 1920, Ruth's first year with the Yankees, he hit 54 home runs. Inside baseball suddenly was dull. Why sweat and work for one run when runs could be had in bunches?

Whack! Two runs. Bam! Three runs.

The public loved it.

Crowds flocked to the Polo Grounds in record numbers to see the Yankees shatter by almost 400,000 the old single-season attendance record of 910,000 set by the 1908 Giants.

McGraw seethed. What the public wanted to see was not his inside-baseball exquisite Giants but the parvenu Ruth and the crude Yankee style of big-inning baseball.

By the end of the 1920 campaign McGraw had had enough. He fought back as only a landlord could: He told the Yankees to leave. Nothing personal, mind you, just go away. Play your games anywhere you see fit, just take leave of the Polo Grounds as soon as you can find a new home. As things turned out, the Yankees and Giants won pennants the next three years, setting the stage for one of the great showdowns in baseball history, the World Series of 1923.

The 1921 Series was the first to be played all in one ballpark and the last to be a best-of-nine-games affair. The Yankees started out strongly, winning the first two games. The second game, in which Giants batters were stifled by Waite Hoyt, was particularly mortifying to McGraw. As a Brooklyn teenager, Hoyt had made his major league debut with the Giants in 1918, striking out two in the only inning he worked. But McGraw had cut him. Hoyt subsequently signed with the Red Sox, who sold him to the Yankees, as was their bad habit with their stars. Now he was back at the Polo Grounds.

In the third game an early Yankee lead disappeared, and the Giants won 13-5. That game changed the tone of the Series, and the Giants swept four of the next five. Most important, they had controlled Ruth.

"Ruth! Why all the excitement about Ruth?" McGraw said grouchily afterward. "We've been pitching all along to Rogers Hornsby and he's a three-to-one better hitter than Ruth."

During Ruth's minor league days McGraw had been interested in signing him as a pitcher. Now McGraw was openly contemptuous of the Ruthian style, predicting that the Babe would end up hitting into more double plays than grandstands. And the result of the 1921 Series seemed to bear out Little Napoleon's prediction. Ruth was held to a meaningless homer and four singles. The Giants won the championship; the new slugging style was discredited.

Over the next summer much newspaper space was used to report the insults exchanged by the two sides. McGraw rarely missed an opportunity to slam the Yankees. Whenever Ruth hit a home run with McGraw present, he would turn toward the Giants skipper and bellow, "How's that for a double-play ball, Mac?" But strange as it sounds today, it was the Yankees who always seemed to be swimming upstream. They were still the Giants' tenants, after all. And in 1922 McGraw had made a few subtle moves that transformed his Giants of that year into one of the greatest teams ever.

Heinie Groh had been obtained from Cincinnati to play third base. Groh was a small but powerful man, one of the great bat doctors of all time. He used a 46-ounce bat with a handle that had been shaved down until the whole bat looked like an elongated Bordeaux bottle. The acquisition of Groh enabled Frankie Frisch to move from third base to second, his natural position and a spot where his abilities as a field leader could flourish.

For centerfield, McGraw had rescued Charles Dillon Stengel from the Phillies in mid-1921. In 1922 McGraw used him well, platooning him in center with Bill Cunningham. But almost more important was Stengel's other role. He would sit on the bench beside McGraw, developing strategies and serving as a coach without portfolio. It was here that Casey acquired the *saber hacer* that later served him as a manager.

In the 1922 Series, McGraw again found ways to handle Ruth. What the methods lacked in subtlety they made up for in effectiveness. Ruth saw little but low, outside curveballs for the entire Series. And he heard little but epithets from the Giants' infielders—racial epithets. There were not many ways to get the Bambino riled, but one of them was to suggest that his physical prowess—baseball and otherwise—stemmed from African ancestry.

Ruth took the bait. He was so distracted that he hit .118 for the Series.

Not surprisingly, the Giants swept the Series. Once again McGraw's style of baseball seemed vindicated. The Yankees had been easily dispatched twice, and now McGraw had what appeared to be an added bonus. The Yankees were leaving the Polo Grounds, although not quite in the way the Giants had envisioned. By evicting the Yankees the Giants had hoped to send them wandering around the city, eventually to settle in some shabby digs, presumably in a remote section of Queens, such as the Corona Ash Dump, depicted as the "valley of ashes" in F. Scott Fitzgerald's *The Great Gatsby*, where eventually Shea Stadium and Citi Field would stand, or rise from the ashes, depending how you wanted to see it.

Instead, Yankee Stadium rose in full view of the Polo Grounds, on a tract of land across the Harlem River purchased from the Astor Estate. Yankee owner Jacob

Ruppert had rushed the stadium to completion in less than a year.

It was there in 1923 that the real Giants-Yankees showdown finally took place, at least for this era.

McGraw went into the 1923 Series on the threshold of his most cherished goal: three consecutive world championships. All that his Giants had to do was beat a team they had already handled in 1921 and 1922. But first there had to be a few introductory hostilities between the clubs.

This time the center of the storm was 20-year-old Lou Gehrig. McGraw's scouts had spotted Gehrig in the summer of 1921, just before he entered Columbia University on a football scholarship. Through some quick talking they had signed him to a professional baseball contract and hidden him at the Eastern League's Hartford club under another name—not an uncommon practice of the day. But a former A's and Highlanders hurler named Andy Coakley, who was then the Columbia baseball coach, got wind of the move. Coakley went to a Hartford game to confront Gehrig. "What," he demanded, "are you doing in that uniform?"

Coakley dragged Gehrig back to New York, saved his scholarship and extricated him from the Hartford contract. Gehrig played football and baseball for Columbia; then the Yankees signed him in the spring of 1923. Where did they send him? To Hartford, of course. He tore up the league. The Yankees brought him up at the end of the year, and he hit .423 in 13 games. It appeared that they had another treasure.

But Gehrig had not moved up to the big club until after Sept. 1, which meant that he was ineligible for the Series. Coincidentally, first baseman Wally Pipp had suffered a painful rib injury. The Yankees requested that Gehrig take Pipp's place on the World Series roster. Baseball commissioner Kenesaw Mountain Landis responded that Gehrig could play only if the opposing manager consented.

Fat chance of that happening!

McGraw, keeping the events of 1921 in mind, was quite happy to withhold consent. First Hoyt had gotten away to the Yankees. Next Ruth. Now Gehrig. It was all too much for McGraw.

"The hazards of baseball," he said. "The rules are quite specific," which, by the way, they were.

Gehrig was not allowed to play, Pipp was patched up, and the World Series of 1923 began.

So disdainful was McGraw of everything connected with the Yankees that he refused to use the new Yankee Stadium locker rooms. His players could change sweatshirts in the stadium's clubhouse, nothing more. For Yankee home games McGraw's troops used their locker room at the Polo Grounds, then took cabs across the Harlem River into enemy territory.

In the ninth inning of the opening game with the score tied at 4-4, Stengel hit what might have been a single to left center. Leftfielder Bob Meusel had been guarding the line. Centerfielder Whitey Witt had been shifted toward right. Before anyone could quite figure out how it had happened, the ball was between them, hopping toward the wall 450 feet away, and Casey was running the bases as if his life depended on it. Because anything involving Stengel had to have a comic touch, he was cheering himself on at the same time, yelling, "Go on, Casey, go on!"

Damon Runyon immortalized the incident in the New York *American* the next day. Rounding second, Stengel felt a sponge break free inside his left shoe. Rounding third, he wobbled like a cripple. Sliding home, he signaled himself safe. Fortunately, umpire Billy Evans agreed. Ruth had been deprived of hitting the first World Series home run at Yankee Stadium. And the Giants had the run that would win Game 1.

Yes, 1923 looked like a replay of the previous two years.

But, as Heywood Broun wrote in the New York *World* the following day, "The Ruth is mighty and shall prevail."

True enough. In the second game, at the Polo Grounds, Ruth walked in the first, and then in the fourth he caught a Hugh McQuillan curveball and belted it over the right-field grandstand.

Ruth came up again in the fifth. Walk him? McGraw had answered that question before the game. "Why shouldn't we pitch to him?" said John J. "We pitch to better hitters in the National League."

Oh? Giants reliever Jack Bentley showed the Babe a slow curve. Ruth showed Bentley a fierce line drive into the lower deck. The Yankees had a 4-1 lead and the game. And the tide seemed to be turning. The Babe was starting to catch up to Giants pitching.

The unexpected hero in the third game was again Stengel. In the seventh inning Casey—who hit with surprising power during his career—lined a ball into the right-field seats at Yankee Stadium. It would prove to be the only run of the game but not the only fun. The target of relentless heckling from the Yankee dugout, Stengel turned toward the Yankee bench and appeared to be flicking a fly off his nose with the tip of his thumb. But 62,430 people saw Casey's gesture of ill will.

Ruppert later demanded that Stengel be punished, but commissioner Landis refused.

"Casey Stengel," Landis said with uncharacteristic understatement, "can't help being Casey Stengel." Even the Bambino, one of the targets of Stengel's nose thumbing, was amused.

"I didn't mind it," Ruth said. "Casey's a lot of fun."

The Giants had a 2-1 lead in the Series. What followed was the equivalent of an old wall crumbling as a

relentless tide rushes through. Game 4, played at the Polo
Grounds on Oct. 13, was a watershed for professional
baseball.

In the second inning the Yankees finally went to
work on McGraw's pitchers, scoring six runs to move the
game out of reach early. It was 8-0 when the Giants finally
rallied in the bottom of the eighth, but they fell short by
four runs.

"It was a bad game for a good team to lose,"
McGraw remarked when it was over. But maybe he sensed
something, too, because the fifth game, played at Yankee
Stadium, was also a rout, 8-1 in favor of the Yankees. The
American Leaguers scored three runs in the first and four in
the second to make it no contest early on. The turnaround
was absolutely stunning. Forty-eight hours earlier, riding
the heroics of Stengel's second home run, McGraw and his
troops had seemed on the brink of their third straight Series
title. Now their backs were against the wall.

Game 6, at the Polo Grounds, became a classic
struggle between the old baseball and the new. Ruth hit a
home run in the first inning. Then the Giants, playing their
traditional game, chipped away for single runs in four
different innings. The score was 4-1 Giants at the start of
the eighth. That was the Big Inning.

Art Nehf, the Giants pitcher, had been coasting. He
had pitched a shutout only three days earlier, but now in the
eighth, Yankees Wally Schang and Everett Scott both
singled. Then Nehf walked two pinch hitters on eight
pitches, forcing in a run. He had lost his stuff so quickly
that McGraw hadn't had time to warm up Rosy Ryan, his
best reliever. Ryan had to come in anyway. He walked Joe
Dugan and the Yankees had another run. The score was 4-
3, and Ruth was up next.

Somehow, Ryan managed to pull himself together.
In the final gasp of old time, inside baseball, Ryan fanned
Ruth. Perhaps he then thought the worst was over and that

96

the Giants could hold on. If so, he thought wrong. There was no Gehrig to follow Ruth yet—McGraw had seen to that—but there was Meusel, who bounced a ball over Ryan's head.

When Bill Cunningham kicked the ball around in centerfield, the three men already on base scored. The Yankees had five runs in the inning, and 25 minutes later they returned to Yankee Stadium with their first world championship.

McGraw was strangely gracious and philosophical when it was over. "The best team won," he allowed. "The old guard changes but never surrenders."

McGraw must have had an inkling of time passing him by. At 50 he was old beyond his years—his face lined, his hair white and his waistline thick. Worse, McGraw must have known how the public would interpret the 1923 World Series: The mighty Giants had been dethroned by the sluggers from the Bronx. By the next season young players across the land would be holding big bats down by the knob and swinging from the heels.

That is, of course, exactly what happened. The stars who evolved over the next few years were all sluggers: Ruth, Gehrig, Rogers Hornsby, Jimmy Foxx, Hack Wilson, Chuck Klein. Inside baseball was dead. The home run and the big inning—TNT ball, as it was called at the time—had killed it.

McGraw appeared in one more World Series, the following year against Washington. The American League won that one, too. McGraw's teams remained contenders after that, but they would never again finish first.

As for the Yankees, the nucleus was in place for the great, explosive teams that would rule baseball for the next half century. Playing exactly the type of ball that McGraw had so loathed, the Yankees would go on to win 40 pennants and 27 Series titles, much to the dismay of Yankee-haters everywhere. Their park in the Bronx may have been the house that Ruth built, and that George Steinbrenner re-built, but John J. McGraw, the perfect foil, had certainly laid the foundation.

An Ebbets Field Reminiscence

When my father first went over to the Dodgers there was serious concern about a Maglie/Robinson feud. Yet Robinson and Furillo, I think, were the first ones to greet and welcome him. He figured it would be a battle just getting there. Considering his battles with Robinson, that was a HUGE deal. The rest of the team immediately followed suit.

The fans, on the other hand, took a while. I met many Dodger fans as a kid who told me they hated him, and it took a good portion of the (1956) season to give him his due. He would have been better in those middle years if it wasn't for the back injury. Didn't get it repaired until he went to the Dodgers. His back was fixed by a hometown doctor during the off season and no one knew, so the Dodgers picked him up cheap, which turned out to be a great investment....

I know a story of (him) throwing an entire room service cart out of their hotel window, but don't remember who the roommate was. One day on the road Dad wanted to go to a certain restaurant after showering, but his roommate had already ordered room service for them both. When the food showed up, Dad pushed it out to the balcony and threw it over the railing down to the pool area. Problem solved, let's go eat.

He never was a baseball player to me. He was just Dad. One day in an airport, I was maybe 11 or 12 and some guy saw my name and started talking about Dad, his great career, etc. Then he asked me, "He's a southpaw right?" I said yeah. I didn't even know what a southpaw was. I don't know why that stuck with me all these years, but it really shows how much I didn't care back then. Took me a LONG TIME to finally give him his due in my heart.

Joe Maglie
Jacksonville, Arkansas
June 2019

Photo of Joe Maglie at Ebbets Field, circa 1956, courtesy of Joe Maglie.

Chapter 7 – The Long Reign of King Carl

Joe DiMaggio faced hundreds of pitchers in his career, but there was no question of who was the toughest. Joe said it many times: Carl Hubbell, whom DiMaggio faced in the 1936 and 1937 World Series. The 1930's was Hubbell's decade as the dominant hurler in American baseball.

How dominant was he? The numbers make the jaw drop.

He led the National League in innings pitched in 1933 with 308. He led the league in strikeouts in 1937 with 159. He led the league in shutouts in 1933 with 10. He compiled a streak of 461⁄3 scoreless innings and four shutouts in 1933. On May 8, 1929 he pitched an 11-0 no-hitter against Pittsburgh, then, as an encore, pitched an 1-0 18-inning shutout against the St. Louis Cardinals on July 2, 1933. This was a hitter's era, but not when Hubbell was on the mound.

More? Sure.

Hubbell was twice the National League MVP, in 1933 and 1936. He led the league in wins 3 times: in 1933 with 23, in 1936 with 26, and in 1937 with 22. He led the N.L. in ERA three times in 1933 with 1.66, 1934 with 2.30, and in 1936 2.31.

DiMaggio knew a thing or two about batting…and streaks.

Similarly, Hubbell knew something about pitching…and streaks.

On July 17, 1936, the lefthanded Hubbell improved his record to 11-6 by defeating the Pittsburgh Pirates 6-0. Hubbell was doing all he could to keep his fifth-place team alive in the National League pennant race. Five hits, no walks and two strikeouts.

"Great game, Carl," the fans shouted.

Two days later Hubbell appeared in relief to beat Cincinnati. Then, without missing his regular turn, he started again on July 21 and pitched a 10-inning, complete-game victory over the Cardinals. King Carl had begun the greatest individual winning streak in baseball history.

By Aug. 2, 1936, Hubbell had won 5 in a row. By the first week of September the streak was 11, including 2 victories over each of the league's top teams, the Cardinals, Pirates and Cubs. Hubbell's screwball, a lefthanded version of Christy Mathewson's old fadeaway, was hopping as never before. In a repertoire that also included a respectable fastball and a sharp curve, the pitch bordered on the unhittable.

Hubbell had perhaps as good a control of his pitches as any man who ever pitched. While he was growing up on his family's Missouri farm, he "practiced for hours," he used to explain, "throwing stones at a barn door until I could hit knotholes no bigger than a dime."

Hubbell had used the screwjie to strike out Babe Ruth, Lou Gehrig, Jimmie Foxx, Al Simmons and Joe Cronin consecutively in the 1934 All Star Game. Batters didn't see it very often, and when they did, they didn't connect solidly. Let's face it: these were pretty good results for a pitch the Detroit Tigers had urged Hubbell to discard at a tryout camp eight years earlier.

According to accounts of the day, the Tigers released Hubbell due to Ty Cobb's opinion of the screwball as a pitch that would eventually wreck his arm. It looked like a curve on the way to the plate, then broke in the opposite direction. John McGraw, who never cared much for Cobb anyway, cared even less for Cobb's opinion and approved the signing of Hubbell for the Giants.

About that screwball: In throwing a standard curveball, a left-handed pitcher twists his wrist to the left in a counter-clockwise motion, with the pitch breaking in toward a left-handed batter. Hubbell's screwball forced him to defy nature by twisting his wrist to the right, causing the pitch to break down and to the left, away from the right-handed batter. Thrown properly, Hubbell's signature pitch confounded the hitters but also resulted in considerable strain on his left elbow. Many years later, Hubbell confessed that the pitch had begun to hurt his elbow as early as 1934. By 1938, the pain was excruciating.

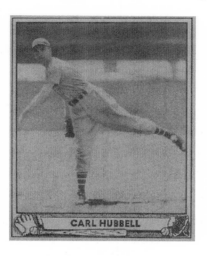

CARL HUBBELL

In addition to "King Carl," the sportswriters of the era nicknamed Hubbell "Old Long Pants" or "The Meal Ticket." Bob Broeg, the great St. Louis-based sportswriter was more specific in his description. "Hubbell is awkwardly angular, gaunt, lean-visaged, and almost Lincolnesque in appearance," he wrote, "with no hips, less derriere, and the longest shinbones in captivity."

In late September, Hubbell's streak reached 16, and the Giants roared past the top three contenders to win the pennant by five games. Of the 16 wins, one was in relief and 14 were complete games. Hubbell's ERA for the stretch was 1.86.

Hubbell continued his mastery in the opening game of the World Series, defeating the Yankees, 6-1. But then inevitably he lost, dropping the fourth game 5-2 as the Yankees took the Series four games to two.

Hubbell's regular-season streak was still alive, however, and for Giants fans and baseball historians, that was all that mattered. The streak became the hot topic of the Hot Stove League. With 16 in a row, Hubbell had taken aim at one of baseball's oldest records. Two former Giants had won 19 games in a row—Tim Keefe in 1888 and Rube Marquard in 1912. People began to ask: If Hubbell won four straight to start the 1937 season, would he have the new record?

Marquard, who had retired after the 1925 season, certainly had an opinion. He replied sourly that his streak was actually 20. He contended that an official scorer had robbed him of an extra victory in 1912.

The debate intensified after Hubbell opened the 1937 season with a 3-0 victory over the Boston Braves. But then Ford Frick, the president of the National League, stepped in. He ruled that the record could be broken only by a pitcher who won more than 19 games in a single season. Yes, this is the same Ford Frick who, as the commissioner of baseball, ruled in 1961 that Roger Maris could receive full credit for breaking Babe Ruth's home run record only by exceeding 60 home runs within 154 games.

Well, a ruling was a ruling, and that was the end of that. The press and the public promptly lost some interest in King Carl's streak now that it was officially back at one. So Hubbell just went out and threw. His next start was an 11-2 laugher against the Dodgers, which if you were still counting, made 18. But was anybody counting?

Then came trouble. "There is always a game you're destined to lose, where the ground ball goes to the wrong place or your side doesn't get the big hit," the 83-year-old Hubbell recalled when interviewed at his home in Arizona in 1988. "I had one of those games against the Reds."

On May 4, Hub was coasting 7-0 over Cincinnati in the middle innings when the magic failed. The Reds rocked him for six runs and sent him to the showers with two out and one on base in the seventh. But relief specialist Harry Gumbert came in to subdue the rally and hold Cincinnati scoreless the rest of the way. Yes, it had been one of those games a man seemed fated to lose—but Hubbell had won it, anyway.

That made it Nineteen.

Now there was no stopping him. He beat the Cubs, Pirates and Cardinals. Then Dick Coffman came in to get a final out and snuff the Pirates. Twenty-three and counting. A relief win against Cincinnati made it 24. It was becoming clear: Carl Hubbell would never lose another game for as long as he lived.

Or so it seemed.

On a sweltering Memorial Day in 1937 the Giants were scheduled to play a holiday doubleheader as part of their annual gang war with the crosstown Brooklyn Dodgers. The public had taken notice.

By 12:30 that afternoon the New York City Fire Department had already closed the Polo Grounds gates. Twenty-five thousand ticketless fans were turned away, while 61,756 packed the stands. Some were nestled into the rafters of the upper deck. Every one of them seemed to scream when Hubbell threw his first pitch: a ball ominously far off the plate. Then he threw three more. An infield hit followed, then a sacrifice. A ground ball brought in one run and a triple another to make it 2-0, Brooklyn.

Giants fans fell strangely silent.

In the park that day was a pudgy country kid from Trauger, Pennsylvania named Paul Chervinko. He was seeing his first major league game from an exceptionally good vantage point. He was the Dodgers' catcher.

Chervinko would amass a prodigious total of 11 hits and five RBIs in a major league career that would span 42 games. He was exactly the type of inexperienced batter Hubbell normally retired on three strikes...when the screwball was screwballing. That day it wasn't.

In the third inning, in a key play in the game, Chervinko lined a solid single to right field with the bases loaded. Forty percent of his career RBIs scored, nudging the game out of reach. It ended 10-3, Dodgers. The streak was dead at 24. The firemen had barred the wrong people from the Polo Grounds. They should have locked out the Dodgers.

In a prearranged ceremony, Babe Ruth—looking very blimpish in his baggy tan suit—presented Hubbell the 1936 MVP trophy between games of the doubleheader. The pitcher graciously appeared and acknowledged a thunderous ovation.

Nobody was more grateful than the Giants players. Thanks to the Meal Ticket, they were headed for their second straight World Series, and for a ballplayer in the Great Depression, that was the only place to be.

"During the 1930's, no one was making much money," King Carl remembered years later. "My top salary was $22,500 in 1936. So the World Series was it. Get in and make some extra money."

The World War Two years were cruel to the New York Giants. Hubbell posted a 4–4 record in 1943, marking the only time he didn't record double-digit wins. Alas, the curse of Ty Cobb finally came down upon Hubbell. After years of throwing his screwball, he had a deformed left hand with the palm facing away from his body instead of toward it.

The team released him. However, Giants owner Horace Stoneham named Hubbell director of player development, a post he would hold for 35 years. During that time, he lived in New Jersey. He stayed there after the Giants defected to San Francisco. The last years of his life were spent as a Giants scout, even as he lived into his eighties. His number 11 which he wore most of his career was retired by the Giants in 1944. He was elected to the National Baseball Hall of Fame in 1947.

In his later years, Hubbell looked back with justifiable pride upon baseball's greatest sustained pitching performance. But he also frequently said, "I never tried to set any streaks or go for any kind of record. It just happened."

Something else happened years later. Frick's 1937 ruling that had prevented Hubbell's accomplishment from entering the record books was rescinded in 1974. Though 19 victories remains as the single-season standard, baseball's Rules Committee officially acknowledged Hubbell's streak as the longest ever.

"For 37 years they kept me in limbo," Hubbell chuckled shortly before his death in a motor vehicle accent in Scottsdale, Arizona in 1988. "But today it counts."

Hubbell's winning streak has proved to be one of the most enduring achievements in baseball history. The closest anyone has come to breaking it was the 22-game streak that Pittsburgh reliever Roy Face put together in 1958 and '59.

But there was a footnote to the record in which Hubbell took special pride. "During those 24 straight," he would always remind people, "I also had four saves."

"I hated the Yankees and Dodgers and wound up managing both."

Joe Torre

Chapter 8 - Mr. Shibe's Spiteful Fence

Do you like baseball the way it is played at Fenway Park, with the Green Monster looming behind every pitch? If you do, then you would have loved Philadelphia's Shibe Park some 60 years ago. There, out in right field, was the most controversial fence in baseball.

When Shibe Park, home of Connie Mack's world-renowned Philadelphia Athletics, opened on April 12, 1909, the distance down the right field foul line was 360 feet. In the era of the dead baseball, rarely did the ball travel that far. (Pick up a bat sometime and try to hit a croquet ball that distance in the air. Then you'll have the idea.) Indeed, the coziest aspect of the Shibe Park "wall" was its height: 12 feet. It was high enough to block the view of passersby and just far enough from the plate to keep most long drives inside the ballpark. But from the second-story windows and the rooftops of the houses across North 20th Street, spectators had a perfect view of all the A's home games. Therein lies an unusual story.

By the 1920's, Shibe Park's grandstands had been rebuilt and home plate relocated. The distance down the right field line was now 329 feet. And by then, the game of baseball had changed. The cork-centered ball was in use, trick pitches like the spitter were banned, and the big lefthanded hitters of the day - notably Babe Ruth and Lou Gehrig - spent many afternoons blasting baseballs over friendly fences in Shibe and a few other parks.

The results were dramatic: In 1918, the last-place A's led the league in home runs with 22. Four years later, the seventh-place A's led with 111 home runs, thanks to the 12-foot wall and an early slugger named Tillie Walker who had also joined Babe Ruth as a co-home run champion of the American League with the staggering total of 11.

Many years later, in 1987, Roger (Doc) Cramer, then 82, then residing in Beach Haven, N.J., recalled the right field situation. Cramer played in 2,239 American League games between 1929 and 1948, and for four years he was Mack's regular centerfielder.

"It was a bad wall to play," he remembered. "It had concrete sticking out and would stop you right quick if you ran into it. Worse, there were no caroms. The ball would drop straight down."

Also in 1987, Edwin (Dib) Williams, then 77, a regular infielder for Connie Mack during the glory days, recalled another feature of the wall. It brought people into the game.

Literally.

"Kids on North 20th Street," Williams said from his home in Greenbrier, Arkansas, "used to shove ladders up against the other side, scale the wall and disappear into the grandstands." During games, other kids would sit on top of the wall and no one bothered them.

Some of the players also liked the wall. George "Mule" Haas and Mickey Cochrane hit directly at it. Or over it. Al Simmons and Jimmie Foxx, righthanded batters, were so strong that they could easily target an outside pitch for North 20th Street. Obviously, it was an interesting block on which to live. You just had to pay attention.

"I saw Foxx hit balls into the windows across the street," Williams remembered, "and I saw Ruth hit them over the rooftops." This was powerhouse baseball. Balls would crash down in this otherwise peaceful North Philadelphia neighborhood dozens of times each week. But in the entrepreneurial spirit of the day, the frequent sound of a baseball crashing against a front porch or bedroom wall was not a nuisance; it was the sound of opportunity knocking.

"Admission to the bleachers at Shibe Park was 50 cents when I was a boy," recalled John J. Rooney, a professor at La Salle University in Philadelphia. "But at our house and on our rooftop, where we had a perfect view of the field, the price was only a quarter."

Rooney's family was one of many along North 20th Street that went into business. Anything from dining-room chairs to crates was placed on the rooftops for the paying customers. For the big games with the Yankees, when the 33,608 seats in Shibe Park were sold out, the price of admission was as much as half a dollar. The rooftop business might have seemed like a nickel-and-dime enterprise, but the A's played 77 home games a year and that made for a lot of change.

Then came 1929. Connie Mack had put together one of his finest clubs. Mickey Cochrane was his catcher. The outfield was as good as any in the majors with Al Simmons, Haas and Miller. Jimmie Foxx was the first baseman. Max Bishop was at second and Jimmy Dykes was at third. The Philadelphia A's had their greatest season ever, finishing 18 games in front of the second-place Yankees. Seats on the rooftops sold briskly, as you might imagine.

On Oct. 14, Mule Hass dropped a lazy two-run, ninth-inning homer over the friendly right field wall to tie the fifth game of the World Series against the Chicago Cubs. Simmons doubled off the adjacent scoreboard. Foxx was walked intentionally. Bing Miller doubled off the same scoreboard, and the A's won 3-2 and took the Series four games to one. Sensing the birth of a dynasty, the homeowners across the street erected bleachers—that's right, bleachers—on their rooftops for the following season.

The A's repeated as world champions in 1930 and won the pennant in 1931. Rooftop business was booming, despite the Depression. Fire inspectors went door-to-door suggesting that rooftop seating was a fire hazard and city tax collectors followed, maintaining that the seating created a "place of public amusement."

This was Philadelphia, so greasing a few palms solved the problems and kept almost everyone happy. But there was another cloud on the horizon, a man by the name of John Shibe, part owner (along with his brother, Tom, and Connie Mack) of both the team and the ballpark. He was one of the people who was not happy. In fairness, it should be noted that gate receipts were a ball club's sole source of revenue in those days, aside from selling players.

"John Shibe liked to yell a lot," recalled Cramer with a laugh. "He didn't even like you to walk on the grass behind home plate during batting practice. Didn't want you cutting his turf with your spikes. Oh, he'd holler at you!"

Imagine how a man who didn't want his champion players walking on his grass would react to people scaling his fence with ladders, sitting in someone else's bleachers and even eating hot dogs ("We'd buy them from street vendors for a nickel and sell them on the rooftops for a dime," said Rooney) without his getting a piece of the action.

Shibe was furious. In 1932 he decided to act.

At first he proceeded cautiously. After all, the A's had deep roots in the community. Dib Williams still remembered rooming at Mrs. Truitt's boardinghouse across the street from the park. Several other players took their meals there. Simmons rented a room on the North 20th Street block, stayed in it a few seasons, then continued to pay for it after he was a star and had moved to a downtown hotel.

"Al Simmons was superstitious and didn't want to break his good luck," Williams recalled with a chuckle.

Unfortunately, it was the team that started to run out of luck. The A's were second in the American League in 1932 and third in 1933. Despite some excitement at Shibe Park (Gehrig's four-home run game and Foxx's 58-homer season in 1932), the A's were obviously slipping. They hit the second division in 1934.

Community relations weren't exactly leading the league, either. The homeowners on North 20th, pleading free enterprise, refused Shibe's suggestion that they open the rooftops only when the ballpark was full. So, during the winter of 1934-35, Shibe called carpenters and ironworkers to Shibe Park. Up went a huge expanse of corrugated metal that added 38 feet to the existing 12-foot fence, completely blocking the view from across the street.

It was a jolting thing to see, a blight on the landscape. "We came back from spring training and there it was," Cramer remembered.

"We were out of business on Opening Day, 1935," recalled Rooney.

A series of unsuccessful lawsuits followed, and eventually the rooftop bleachers were taken down. But the great Philadelphia Athletics also came down. In various deals, Cochrane, Cramer, Jimmy Dykes, Foxx, Lefty Grove, Haas, Miller, Simmons and Williams were traded off, mostly for cash and warm bodies.

Attendance at Shibe Park hit the skids: 233,000 for the season, averaging out to about 3000 per game. It could have been worse. The St. Louis Browns drew 80,922 for the season and had one game against the A's at home at which the announced attendance was "300".

The A's hit the American League basement in 1935 with a 58-91 record and stayed there. The wall became a symbol of the team's collapse.

Dubbed "the spite fence," the monstrous new wall shielded from public view a team that no one wanted to see. As it turned out, the new wall was permanent – it stayed till the Phillies closed the crumbling ballpark in 1970 - but the fans were *not* permanent.

Free to come and go, most of the fans went.

The A's stayed on at Shibe for another 19 painful seasons, playing before vast sections of empty grandstands. The fans, like the bleachers across the street, never came back. The Spite wall or fence may have gone up, but when it did, the entire franchise came tumbling down.

Doc and Dib

Some of this chapter on the spite fence at Shibe Park appeared in a shorter version in *Sports Illustrated* in 1987 when I was contributing articles to that publication. It was then I first became fascinated by the A's rocky history – no pun intended to any movie guy - in Philadelphia.

In researching, I had the pleasure of speaking to Doc Cramer and Dib Williams personally (as well as Dr. Rooney). They were wonderful charming men, well into their later years. Cramer and Williams were among the few living former players who remembered Shibe Park in the 1930's, much less playing for Connie Mack. It was a pleasure to speak with them, one which has lasted until this day. They were generous with their time and reminiscences, so I'd like to add a few words here to perpetuate their memory.

Cramer was not a power-hitter. He was a singles-doubles guy and a very good one. But he liked to tell people about the time he was intentionally walked so the opposing pitcher could pitch to Hank Greenberg.

On September 30, 1945, in St. Louis, Detroit had men on second and third in the 9th, down 3–2. Cramer, with the Tigers at the time, was walked to load the bases and set up a force play at any base. Greenberg followed with a grand slam that won the pennant for the Tigers.

Interviewed by Donald Honig in the 1970s in Honig's wonderful book, *Baseball when the Grass was Real: Baseball from the Twenties to the Forties Told by the Men who Played It*, Cramer told of how he would tease the great Greenberg: "So anywhere I go and Hank is there, I always say, 'You know, once they walked me to get to Hank Greenberg' — and never tell 'em what happened, and then Hank always jumps up and says, 'Hey, tell 'em what happened.' But I never do; I just leave it at that."

In his 20-season career, Cramer batted .296 with 2705 hits, 1357 runs, 37 home runs, 842 RBI, 396 doubles, 109 triples, 62 stolen bases and a .340 on-base percentage in 2239 games. Defensively, he compiled a career .979 fielding percentage. He played for the Athletics, the Red Sox, the Tigers and the Senators. He rarely struck out, leading the AL four times in at strikeouts-per-at-bats and finishing in the top four five other seasons. His 2031 games in center field placed him behind only Tris Speaker (2690) and Ty Cobb (2194) in major league history. His 2705 hits are the most of any player retired before 1975 who has not been elected to the Baseball Hall of Fame. As the Chicago White Sox batting coach from 1951 to 1953, he mentored a young second baseman named Nellie Fox, who often credited Cramer with making him a major league hitter.

Cramer had worked as a carpenter before entering the major leagues. He continued to work as a carpenter during the off-seasons. After leaving baseball, he resumed working full time as a carpenter and home builder.

Dib Williams had a much shorter career but did play in almost 500 games. He joined Connie Mack's Athletics in 1930 and served as a back-up middle infielder. The A's won the pennant with a 102-52 record and the World Series in six games over the St. Louis Cardinals. Williams, still only 20 years old until January 1931, appeared in 67 games and hit for a .262 average (the Athletics as a team hit an impressive .294). He drove in 22 runs and hit his first three home runs, the three-run homer in the July 1 game making all the difference in the 4-1 win over the Tigers. He was on the roster for the World Series but didn't play.

The A's won 107 games in 1931, and won the pennant again, finishing 13 1/2 games ahead of the second-place New York Yankees. Dib Williams got into 86 games and lifted his average to .269. He batted in 40 runs. In July alone, he had a grand slam and a bases-clearing triple. He was 5-for-5 on September 15, in the game the Athletics won to clinch the American League pennant.

The Athletics and Cardinals matched up again in the 1931 World Series. This time St. Louis won in 7 games. Williams played shortstop in every game. One tended to think of him as a good-field-no-hit guy, but in the Series, his fielding was as good as anyone's.

No less an observer that John McGraw commented that Williams had been "as steady as a rock [while making] a dozen brilliant plays...without anything that even looked like an error."

Both men passed away in the 1990's, but I remain grateful for their fascinating recollections about Mr. Mack and the American League in the Twenties, Thirties and Forties.

An Ebbets Field Reminiscence

Ebbets Field. Why did I not go there more often? True, it took three subways from Queens, but I should have gone more, just to look around, engrave every detail.

Still, it stays with me, deep in my psyche. (I'll tell you about my Ebbets Field dream shortly.)

I did see Karl Spooner blaze through like a shooting star in 1954 and I did see Mantle hit a grand-slam in the 1953 Series (the ball got bigger and bigger in the upper deck in left), and Dixie Walker did hit a home run in my first game in 1946, and Jackie Robinson did chat with a couple of us urchins under the stands on a day when he was not playing. But why didn't I go more often?

I feel Ebbets Field sometimes when I am at the lovely Botanical Garden in Prospect Park, a few blocks to the west. My head turns like a compass needle, Ebbets Field as the true North Star. (Brooklyn boy Fred Wilpon, owner of the Mets, once told me he feels the same.) I sometimes drive friends or long-suffering family members around the apartments and point out where the players left the clubhouse and walked along Sullivan Place to the parking lot and kids asked for autographs.

A few years ago I attended a conference at Medgar Evers College, where the room faced onto Montgomery Street. While people spoke, my eyes turned to where the outfield stands once were, where I witnessed Mantle's blast.

I remember being in a dugout at Ebbets Field – but in 1958, after the Dodgers had gone away. I was the student publicist for the Hofstra College baseball team, and our rival, St. John's, was using the ghost ballpark. Most of us had never been in a dugout – the floor is below field level. But you know that. Somebody hit a high popup and our guys leaped up to get a better view and one of them skulled himself on the cement roof. I can still see our coach, Mr. Smith, trying to revive him, with his New England accent, saying, "Son, son, are you all right?" (My guys had hard heads; the sub was fine.)

It made me feel sick in 1960 to see the wrecking ball, tauntingly painted like a baseball. Roy Campanella was there. In a wheelchair.

Being in the dugout probably led to my dream. Decades later, when I was 50 or 60, I dreamed I was in the dugout, a pinch-hitter for the Brooklyn Dodgers, pulling my bat out of the rack, eager to take my swings. What did it mean? Sometimes I think it was because I had become friendly with George Shuba, one of Roger Kahn's "Boys of Summer," and one of the nicest ball players I have ever met. George was often a pinch-hitter, which I think is the genesis of the dream. Of course, in my dream, I never get

to home plate; that is how dreams work. But I can feel
Ebbets Field wrapped around me, my field of dreams.

George Vecsey
New York
June 2019

Much to the horror of Dodger fans, even in memory, the
photograph shows New York Yankee Mickey Mantle's
upper deck grand slam off Dodger pitcher Russ Meyer (not
the film director) in the third inning of the fifth game of
the1953 World Series at Ebbets Field. The Yankees won
11-7. The winning pitcher was Jim McDonald. Who?!?!

For some reason, few people remember him, but he
was a successful starter and reliever for the Yankees for 3
years.

"I had no future with the Dodgers, because I was too closely identified with Branch Rickey. After the club was taken over by Walter O'Malley, you couldn't even mention Mr. Rickey's name in front of him. I considered Mr. Rickey the greatest human being I had ever known."

Jackie Robinson

Chapter 9

Babe Ruth, Democrat...or maybe Republican.

You'll recognize one of the men in this picture from a hundred years ago, but maybe not the other. That's Babe Ruth shaking hands with President Warren Harding. The occasion was an April game at Yankee Stadium in 1923, the Stadium's opening season.

The President looks happy. The Babe, not so much. But at least he's trying and one hopes he washed his paws before the photo op. There's a reason about the funny grin. Harding was a Republican. The Babe was a Democrat, or so he said from time to time. But the backstory was trickier than that.

When Harding had been running for President in 1920, Harding had asked for Ruth's endorsement. The Babe had emerged as a superstar in 1919, after all, winning 9 games as a pitcher and slugging 29 home runs, a new record in the major leagues. Ruth had been quick to reject the offer, however, commenting, "Hell, no, I'm a Democrat."

That might have ended the matter, but it didn't.

Fred Lieb was a Philadelphia-born sportswriter who wrote at various times for the New York *Sun* and the New York *Post*. He covered games at the Polo Grounds with a pantheon of early star baseball writers including Grantland Rice, Heywood Broun and Damon Runyon. The fictional sportswriter named Sam Blake in the great Lou Gehrig bio pic, *The Pride of The Yankees*, was based in Lieb and played by actor Walter Brennan. Lieb was close to Ruth and was later credited with first using the term, "The House that Ruth Built," in reference to the new Yankee Stadium. Also noteworthy in the movie, Babe Ruth played himself, as did Gehrig's teammates: Mark Koenig, Bob Meusel and Bill Dickey.

In a memoir in 1977, Lieb recalled that during the 1920 presidential campaign, he was asked by supporters of Warren Harding to bring Ruth to Harding's home in Ohio for a public endorsement, even though Ruth had already demurred.

Lieb wrote, "If I could bring it off, there was $4,000 in it for Babe and $1,000 for me."

That changed Ruth's mind, according to Lieb. "I'm a Democrat, but I'll go to Warren for the money," Ruth responded, a man apparently of flexible political views at that time. Not long afterwards, the quest for Ruth's endorsement vanished. The Black Sox scandal was in the headlines. Harding's people thought it might be wise to avoid any association with baseball. Babe, meanwhile, took things out on American League pitching and hammered 59 home runs, more than any other team in the American League.

It is doubtful that Ruth would have had much in common with Harding's political philosophy, much less Harding's public persona as the dour fatherly upper crust WASP. Harding, was elected on an anti-booze, anti-immigrant, pro-Christian, anti-women's Suffrage, pro-morality platform.

Ruth was a working class Catholic whose family in Baltimore ran a saloon, where Babe had once tended bar and was known to sample the product. Working class urban Catholics tended to be Democrats in those days. Many big city Democratic machines registered voters in bars.

Never mind the fact that Harding served and consumed booze in the White House and, family values guy as he was, fathered an illegitimate child while in office. He just wasn't Babe's type of guy; anyone could see that. Hence, Ruth's reticence at the photo op at Yankee Stadium.

Up until this time Ruth's political participation was minuscule and hardly impressive. In 1915, when the Suffrage movement was lobbying hard for voting rights for women, some women in the movement in Massachusetts offered to pay Boston Red Sox players for each home run they hit at Fenway Park. In was a public relations scheme for their cause.

The future Sultan of Swat hit one home run in Boston that year. He collected his money, endorsed the Suffrage movement, and most likely headed to a bar and a tobacconist with it and who knew where else.

Then again, there were possible explanations for some sympathy between Warren Harding and Babe Ruth. Harding had played the game while growing up. He was a genuine fan and was part-owner of his local minor league team in Marion, Ohio. He took office in 1921, by which time Ruth was the greatest celebrity in the country. Harding invoked the Babe's image at political events. He challenged Americans to "strive for production as Babe Ruth strives for home runs."

In time, Ruth visited the White House as a guest. According to Washington folklore, when Harding attended a game one steaming day at Griffith Stadium, the gloriously unpolished Ruth was said to have commiserated, "Hot as hell, ain't it, Prez?"

Some accounts, however, have it that Ruth made this comment to Harding's successor, Calvin Coolidge, the frosty New Englander, with whom Ruth's relationship was more distant. It's always possible, of course, that had the opportunities presented themselves, Babe might have said the same to both.

Nonetheless, the Babe whacked the first home run in the new Yankee Stadium in front of the President. Then, as weeks went by, the Harding administration puttered along. Postwar prosperity brought popularity for the President, but it all came to sudden terrible end later that summer of 1923.

Harding had suffered for years from an ill-defined condition then known as "neurasthenia," which was a highfalutin term for exhaustion, both physical and emotional. Some of his doctors warned Harding, while he was still in the U.S. Senate, that his multiple amorous affairs might physically injure his delicate and enlarged heart. And for years, Harding had suffered from shortness of breath, chest pain, and difficulty sleeping unless his head was propped up on a ledge of pillow. He had, in short, all the symptoms of what we now know as congestive heart disease, something much more dire than the aforementioned "neurasthenia."

On the evening of Aug. 2, 1923, at San Francisco's Palace Hotel President Warren G. Harding's wife, Florence, was reading to him from the *Saturday Evening Post*. He liked the article she was concluding.

He said groggily, "That's good, go on."

She did. Moments later, he closed his eyes and died in his bed, the victim of a massive heart attack.

The nation mourned the popular President. Ruth sent the President's widow, Florence, a handwritten condolence note (seen here), describing himself as "a personal friend," and lauding "his many kind acts toward individual players."

Calvin Coolidge served out Harding's first term, then won four years of his own with no help or endorsement from The Babe. Prohibition formed the financial basis of the huge criminal empires of the era, women won the right to vote anyway, the immigration laws didn't work and neither did the tariffs. But the over-inflated economy kept Harding's party in power through the decade.

Coolidge refused to run again in 1928. The GOP turned to Herbert Hoover, the former Secretary of The Treasury. The Democrats nominated a guy whom Ruth could better relate to, Governor Al Smith of New York.

Smith was also a Roman Catholic. His origins on New York's Lower East Side reminded Ruth of his own in Baltimore.

"I wasn't fed with a gold spoon when I was a kid," Ruth wrote a Smith campaign official named Franklin D. Roosevelt. "No poor boy can go any too high in this world to suit me."

Keep in mind also that Ruth's parents signed over custody of their son to the St. Mary's Industrial School for Boys in Baltimore when he was a boy. Babe was raised by the Catholic Church. Therein most likely may have been the strong connection that Ruth felt with Smith.

When baseball's most famous player publicly endorsed Smith, the governor of New York, that fall, he became one of the first modern American sports stars to attempt to lend his popularity to a presidential candidate. Today it is normal for politicians to cozy up to the day's sports heroes. But Ruth was the first baseball star who dealt with a President as a celebrity of near-equal magnitude.

Ruth campaigned with enthusiasm for Al Smith in 1928. He gave speeches, made appearances and endorsed the candidate on the radio. In a national radio address for Smith, Ruth declared "what a wonderful thing it is" that "there is a chance for every boy to get to the top in America."

Not everyone saw it the way Ruth did.

The Ku Klux Klan, ever reliable as a pack of bigots, held anti-Smith anti-Catholic cross burnings across the country in protest of Smith's nomination. American Protestants, some of the extremist ones anyway, put forth the belief that a Catholic would be more loyal to the Pope than to the United States. Strange as it sounds these days, the anti-Catholic hate stuff was a political live wire until John F. Kennedy, a Roman Catholic, was elected in 1960.

During the Smith campaign in September 1928, Babe's nose got further ensnarled in Presidential politics.

At Griffith Stadium in Washington, Ruth blew off the opportunity to pose for a photograph with the Republican candidate, Herbert Hoover.

"Nothing doing," the Babe reportedly grumbled. "I'm for Al Smith."

Also in 1928, the poet Carl Sandburg asked Ruth which of all the presidents was "the best model for boys to follow." Ruth replied, "President Wilson was always a great friend of mine."

By coincidence, perhaps, Wilson had been the first president to attend a World Series game — in Philadelphia in 1916, between the Phillies and the Red Sox, a match-up that comes around less frequently than Haley's Comet. Ruth, then a 20-year-old rookie pitcher for Boston, did not take the mound that day but saw Wilson.

Ruth may have been for Al Smith in 1928, but millions of other Americans were not. Smith's campaign was a losing hand from the start, thanks to the Three P's: Peace, Prosperity and Prejudice. Smith was also a poor campaigner. His campaign theme song, *The Sidewalks of New York*, had no appeal whatsoever west of Twelfth Avenue. Folks out in the hinterlands listening to his national radio addresses laughed at his Noo Yawk accent. But the Babe forged ahead, a warrior in a losing cause.

According to Leigh Montville's fine 2006 biography of Ruth, *The Big Bam*, after helping his team defeat the Cardinals in the 1928 World Series, Ruth praised Al Smith while speaking in Terre Haute, Indiana. The slugger spoke from the back of the Yankees' train home from St. Louis.

Uh oh.

There was mainly silence from the Midwest crowd. Deafening silence. The crowd wasn't buying it. Babe was in enemy territory and knew it. Ruth responded by calling out, "The hell with you!" and ended his speech.

Eventually the Yankees' victory train chugged into New York, a friendlier area. Three thousand fans jammed Grand Central Station when word hit the streets that the Babe and his entourage had arrived.

Ruth pushed his way through the crowd, assisted by some of New York's Finest. He led several teammates across the street to The Biltmore Hotel to visit, by pre-arrangement, the candidate himself, Al Smith.

Smith was on his way out of town to visit several Southern states where he would end up tanking. Smith greeted the Yankees and proclaimed Ruth as, "the boss of the youth of America."

The boss?

Smith had issues trying not to sound like the big city Tammany Hall Irish pol that he was.

Ready for something oafish and politically incorrect? Of course you are. Babe went on live radio in New York to talk to a national audience. He explained that he was going to vote for Smith. Tony Lazzeri, the great Yankee second basemen was to follow Ruth to the microphone. Apparently, when Babe yielded the microphone, on the air, he said to Lazzeri, "Okay, Tony. Now tell us who you wops are gonna vote for."

Presumably, the Italian-Americans were going to vote the same as their German-American compatriots, or at least the same as the Babe.

Smith lost the 1928 election. He even lost his home state of New York. But the Babe exacted his get-even moment later on when a reporter asked him if it was right for him to be earning more money than President Hoover, who defeated Smith.

"Why not?" he famously responded. "I had a better year than he did."

Presidents had their way of finding Ruth, rather than the other way around.

During the 1932 presidential campaign, Franklin Roosevelt, who was running against Hoover, attended Game 3 of the World Series between the Cubs and the Yankees at Wrigley Field in Chicago. There Roosevelt witnessed the scene in which the Babe, at least by legend, pointed at the center-field bleachers and then slugged the ball there for a home run.

A few months later, while hosting a White House reception, the victorious Roosevelt threw his arm around Ruth and "complained" that in 1920 when FDR was running for vice president, the Babe's presence in a hotel lobby had diverted the attention of an audience while he was trying to make a speech. Presumably, the Babe was amused.

While Roosevelt's personal charm lasted a lifetime with some people, it was not so with the Babe. In October 1944, nine years after his retirement as a player, with a wartime President Roosevelt seeking a fourth term, Ruth turned his back on the Democrats. He said the country needed "a new pitcher" in the White House.

Registering to vote for the first time in many years, he told reporters, "Mr. Roosevelt is a great man, but we have got to have a change," adding that the president's opponent, Gov. Thomas Dewey of New York, had "done a

good job" in Albany. Later, Ruth attended an election-eve
Madison Square Garden rally for Dewey. The Babe hailed
his candidate, but it didn't accomplish much. FDR won a
fourth term.

One began to wonder if the Babe's endorsement
was bad luck.

Four years later in June of 1948 Ruth made is final
presidential connection, though he didn't know it at the
time. As The New York *Times* reported, Ruth traveled to
New Haven to donate his black-bound manuscript of *The
Babe Ruth Story* to the Yale library. The film version,
starring William Bendix, was scheduled for release the next
month.

Ruth went to Yale Field before the Princeton game
for a ceremony in which he presented the book to Yale's
23-year-old baseball captain, whom *The Times* called,
"George 'Poppy' Bush of Greenwich."

Clutching a cigar stub with trembling hand, while
some of the grown-ups wept, the now gaunt Ruth stepped
up to the microphone. He turned to "Captain Bush," as he
called him. He spoke in a halting voice. He explained that
his book "has a lot of fun in it, and a lot of laughs, a lot of
crying, too."

Poppy, better known as George Herbert Walker
Bush, remembered the incident all his life, remarking
frequently that, "It was obvious that (Ruth) was dying of
cancer, but some of the young, free-spirited 'Babe' was still
there."

True enough, Ruth died two month later on August
16, 1948 at Memorial Sloan Kettering Cancer Center in
Manhattan. He was fifty-three years old. Forty years later,
Poppy was elected President of the United States.

Chapter 10

Lee Grissom, The Superhero in the Crosley Field Rowboat

Okay, what does a guy in a rowboat – seen here in his brief tenure with the Brooklyn Dodgers - on a flooded baseball field have to do with a horror comic? Or even a superhero?

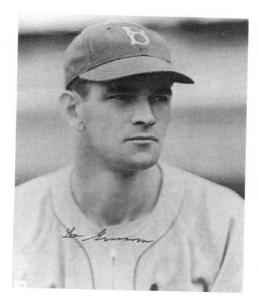

Good question. Here's the answer.

In Cincinnati in 1937 heavy rains caused the Ohio River to flood much of the city, submerging Crosley Field's playing surface – home of the Reds - under 21 feet of water. During a two-week period in January the Cincinnati area received six to twelve inches of rain, causing the Ohio River to crest and submerge Crosley Field. The flood waters were high enough to bury the outfield walls. Damage to the ballpark was minimal, but the deluge allowed Reds pitcher Lee Grissom to take a rowboat with head groundskeeper Matthias Schwab and row over the fences and into the ballpark, as evidenced here. Why miss a photo op, right?

Here we see Cincy Reds pitcher Lee Grissom and head groundskeeper Matty Schwab cross the field in a rowboat.

Grissom (whose younger brother Marv Grissom was also a major league pitcher, mostly with the New York Giants) had a unique status in baseball having nothing to do with the game, but everything to do with comic art.

Follow this along.

Lee Grissom had been born in Texas but grew up on a farm in California. Never much of one for books 'n' learnin', he was more a guy who showed a penchant for drinkin' 'n' fightin'. He never played baseball in high school because he never went to high school, opting out to work on the family farm. He was a big kid, however, and soon became a solid local ball player. Eventually, he was spotted by a former minor-league player and manager named Gene Valla. Valla gave Lee a job in his tire shop, coached him personally and gave him a chance to play semipro ball in San Francisco. Eventually, he found his way into the Cincinnati farm system, pitched well and, at age 26, made his major-league debut in 1934 in a relief outing.

Big kid? Now at six-foot-three and two hundred pounds, he was a very large kid. He made his first major-league start at Brooklyn's Ebbets Field on September 11, 1934 against the Dodgers and couldn't get anyone out. He gave up two hits, walked one, and allowed three runs. He was tagged with the loss in his only major-league decision of the year.

In 1935 Grissom was back in the minors. He was 13-13 pitching for the Fort Worth Cats in the Class A Texas League. In September, he was called up again with the Reds and this time got a few people out. He started three September games, with one win, one loss, and one no-decision.

Future major leaguer? Well, maybe.

The Reds hoped he would be a starter in 1936 but a holdout and an illness sabotaged his season. He continued to get good press: *The Sporting News* praised Grissom as "tall, powerful, cocky, and armed with a crackling fastball." In January of 1937 the Reds brought him to Cincinnati to undergo more medical treatment, which is why he happened to be there for the Great Ohio River Flood of 1937.

Perhaps all that water helped. Grissom throughout his life had problems with wildness: both on the mound and in terms of his own self-discipline. As good as his "crackling" fastball was, frequently no one had any idea where it was going to go, including the guy who threw it. It was prone to crackling outside the plate. And Lee was given to brawls, bar rooms and so on.

Nonetheless, the 1937 season was Grissom's best year in baseball. Pitching as a starter and sometimes from the bull pen, he led the National League in shutouts, was second in strikeouts per innings pitched, and third in saves. He was picked for the All Star Game at Griffith Stadium,

Washington, D.C. by New York Giants manager Bill Terry. He entered the summer classic in the fifth inning and struck out the first two batters he faced, Lou Gehrig and Earl Averill. He then coughed up consecutive doubles to Joe Cronin and Bill Dickey before retiring Sam West on a fly ball. Commendable!

Grissom had high hopes for 1938, but once again bad luck found him. Early in the season he broke an ankle in a stolen base attempt. The injury cost him his season and possibly cost the 1938 Reds a pennant.

But also in June of 1938, the year after the flood, and not long after the broken ankle, came the first issue of *Action Comics*. The Numero Uno issue of *Action Comics* introduced the character Superman and started a superhero craze, not to mention phrases like "truth, justice and the America way" and "faster than a speeding bullet." In the last section of the first edition of the comic – a section called *'Odds'n'Ends'* - were cartoons on a single page depicting sports heroes. Included were four baseball players – Babe Ruth, Lou Gehrig, Sam Leslie, and…. The same Lee Grissom seen rowing across Crosley Field, slower than a speeding bullet.

Why? Because Grissom too wanted to be a superguy.

Grissom had frequently expressed the desire to pitch both ends of a doubleheader. But forget about that. In the eight decades since it was published, the first issue of the comic book has become an insanely-prized collectors' item. The back section, Grissom's section, was drawn by an artist named Shelley Moldoff.

Moldoff was best known for his early work on the DC Comics characters Hawkman and Hawkgirl. He was also one of Bob Kane's primary "ghost artists" (a sly term for an uncredited collaborator) on the superhero Batman.

Moldoff co-created the Batman supervillains Poison Ivy, Mr. Freeze, the second Clayface, and Bat-Mite, as well as the original heroes Bat-Girl, Batwoman, and – my favorite just by name alone - Ace the Bat-Hound. Then when superhero comics went out of fashion in the postwar era, Moldoff became an early pioneer in horror comics, packaging two such ready-to-prints titles in 1948, including one gem called, *This Magazine Is Haunted.*

The comic mentioned above, seen here including the *Odd's 'N Ends* page, sold in a 2011 auction for a whopping $2.16 million.

In 1939, Grissom's final season as a Red, he was the fourth starter on a team that won the pennant. He also pitched against the DiMaggio Yankees in the 1939 World Series.

On January 4, 1940, the same New York Yankees acquired Grissom for star reliever Joe Beggs. He appeared in five games for the Yankees, pitched okay but was put on waivers. He was picked up by the Brooklyn Dodgers, won two and lost five for the Brooks but was demoted to the Montreal Royals in the International League. On May 6,

1941 – for a dose a real world horror - he was traded to the Philadelphia Phillies.

The Phillies were beyond terrible that year, as they so often were in their "Phutile Phillies" epoch. Grissom would go 2-13. He made his final appearance on September 24, 1941, at the age of 33. He pitched 7.1 innings in relief against the New York Giants and gave up no earned runs in a mop-up assignment. The Phillies lost that game plus three of the remaining four games on the schedule to set a franchise record of 111 losses in a season. There's an old adage in baseball that maintains that you're going to win a third of your games and lose a third of your games. It's what you do with the remaining third that determines a successful season. The 1941 Phillies seemed intent on losing *all* their games. They finished 19 games out of seventh place, having won all of 43 games.

Then came American entry into World War Two. Grissom enlisted in the US Army and served his country with honor. After the war, he returned home to work at his family's farm and pitch for local teams. But he wasn't finished fighting.

In 1952 he was tried and acquitted of manslaughter for the death of a man during a bar fight in which he threw

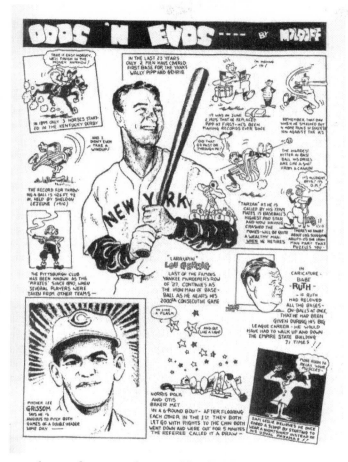

more than a few punches and had more solid hits than in any major league season. He died in Corning, California in 1998 at age 90, about sixty years after he rowed across his home field in Cincy and a year after that comic with his likeness in it sold for all that dough.

Chapter 11 – The Ball That Wouldn't Bounce.

Although I'm too young to remember baseball the way it was played in the spring of 1943, my father used to tell me about it. That was the year the major leagues opened the season with something called a "balata" ball. In fact, balata ball was one of the nicer things the players called it.

It was round and white and had the familiar, reassuring Spalding label, but it sure didn't act like an ordinary baseball. It did bounce, but not very much, and that was the problem. For the first two weeks of the season, a gruesome specter haunted the game: Modern baseball appeared to be on its way back to the pre-1920 dead-ball era. The national pastime, as happens at regular intervals, was imperiled.

To be blunt, 1943 was a horrible year. For the Western democracies, it was the darkest time of the war. Most of Europe was occupied by the enemy and so was most of the South Pacific. But President Franklin D. Roosevelt had decreed that professional baseball could continue; it was good for the morale of the nation, he said. Still, there would have to be certain restrictions. Teams would have to find players among men too young, too old or too infirm for, or temporarily deferred from, the draft. New York teams could play twilight games but not evening games lest the arc lights become landmarks for enemy submarines. And the materials used for equipment could not be essential to the war effort. That, as 1943 fans soon discovered, was where the trouble started.

Though the casual baseball fan probably didn't realize it, the horsehide that Babe Ruth used to bash over fences had come from Belgium and France—where the also-rans of one weekend's tiercé might wind up at the *boucherie de cheval* a few days later. Major league baseball quickly found adequate supplies of Bolivian and domestic horsehide, so one problem—that of the ball's covering—was solved. But an even greater difficulty loomed: a shortage of rubber. Rubber is an essential ingredient of a baseball's core, and it always has been. The core is a cork composition that contains a small percentage of rubber, wrapped by two black rubber shells held in place by another rubber wrapping, which is traditionally red. But when the Japanese seized Malaya and the Dutch East Indies, the U.S. was cut off from its usual source of supply. About a ton of the stuff was required in the construction of a tank and about half that for a long-range bomber. So Uncle Sam banned the use of rubber in all items not essential to the war effort, and that included baseballs.

By the time Billy Southworth's St. Louis Cardinals had disposed of Joe McCarthy's Yankees in the 1942 World Series, the major leagues and A.G. Spalding & Brothers knew they faced a serious problem. Although some clubs still had a few bags of the 1942 balls around, inventories of traditional baseballs were low. A substitute for rubber would have to be found. Commissioner Kenesaw Mountain Landis asked Spalding to come up with something, preferably something with a little jackrabbit in it. Averages and slugging percentages had been in decline since 1939, a memorable year for bashing balls over the fences.

As occurs in most times of crisis, a committee was formed. On it were Landis, American League president Will Harridge, and Cincinnati general manager Warren Giles. These three wise men conferred with Spalding over various formulas for a new ball. Spalding did its best and really couldn't be faulted for the events that followed.

On March 13, 1943, five weeks before Opening Day, the new ball was introduced to the press. It looked and felt like a real baseball, but it had a granulated cork center instead of the high-grade cork and rubber mixture, and there was no rubber shell or rubber wrapping around that core. Instead, to give it a little pop, there were two hard shells of a rubberlike substance inside the ball, hugging the core. One shell was red and the other black. For the first time, Americans heard the ominous word "balata," which was what the two shells were made of.

Balata was a non-strategic substance. It is very similar to rubber but lacks rubber's elasticity. Made from the dried juices of certain tropical trees, it was normally used in the manufacture of industrial gaskets and the insulation of telephone lines. Actually, most American sportsmen had already held balata in their hands without knowing it—the hard outer shells of golf balls were, and some still are, made of balata.

Warren Giles paid close attention to the development of the balata ball, and as the opening of the season approached, he was starting to lose sleep. For most of spring training—played in the North that year because of wartime travel restrictions—1942 baseballs had been in play. They were scruffy old ones whose use would save money and resources. But toward Opening Day, balata balls were used in two games between Giles's Reds and the Cleveland Indians.

Over 21 innings, the two teams pounded out a grand total of one extra-base hit. Giles said nothing, crossed his fingers and prayed that what he had really seen was some unexpectedly good pitching. Yet, in his heart, he knew that wasn't so.

On April 21 the umpires shouted, "Play ball!"

And the 16 teams tried. Truly, they tried.

The Cardinals, who had led the National League in almost all offensive categories in 1942, opened their season at Crosley Field in Cincinnati. They lost 1-0 in 11 innings. The next day they did a little better. They lost 1-0 in 10 innings. Witnesses were quick to focus on the problem. The new ball had the spunk and resilience of a croquet ball. It wouldn't go anywhere. Swat it and your hands stung for two minutes. It was like hitting a large stone. If the baseball of the pre-Ruth era was dead, this one was positively embalmed. It should have gone to war as a weapon.

"We knew something was wrong with it," Dodger infielder Frenchy Bordagaray recalled many years later. "But we didn't know what."

Giles knew what. His worst fears were confirmed. As he suspected all along, the ball was a dud, pronounced the deadest they had ever seen by managers Southworth of the Cardinals, Bill McKechnie of the Reds and Leo Durocher of the Dodgers. Dodgers President Branch Rickey was straightforward when asked to comment about the ball.

"Dead?" he said. "Why, that ball was dead at birth!"

After his team lost to Cleveland 1-0 on Opening Day, Tiger manager Steve O'Neill declared, "Any club would be lucky to get two runs in a game with this new ball. It's deader than the one in use when I was playing." O'Neill had been a catcher for the Indians in 1911. So Giles, to a chorus of approval from players and managers, set about to gather evidence and get the balata ball out of play.

Up to the roof of Crosley Field went the G.M., carrying a bag with a dozen balata balls—now in use at all the ball parks—and another sack of good old 1942 Spaldings that had remained in the Reds' equipment room. Giles's head groundskeeper waited on the sidewalk below. Performing a task that could never have been in any general manager's job description, Giles started dropping baseballs off the roof. The groundskeeper carefully measured the bounces off the concrete pavement. On average, an old ball bounced 13 feet in the air. A balata ball bounced 9½ feet. Applying the findings of the great Crosley Field roof-to-sidewalk experiment, Giles judged that the balata ball was 26.9% less resilient than its predecessor.

On another front, sportswriter Hy Turkin of the New York *Daily News* took some balata balls to The Cooper Union for the Advancement of Science and Art, where scientists sliced them, unraveled them and swatted them with wooden mallets. The verdict: 25.9% less resilience. The finding was remarkably similar to that from the Cincinnati test. And what did it mean in practice? Simply this: The monster 400-foot home run of 1942 was now the lazy 300-foot fly of 1943. Happy outfielders were easily reeling in what should have been goners.

But what could be done? Major league games resembled replays of the 1905 World Series, in which every game was a shutout.

The Reds and the Cardinals concluded a four-game series with six runs scored. Total. Combined. Eleven of the first 29 games played in the two leagues were shutouts, a record. Seven of those were "low hitters," with three safeties or fewer by at least one club. The Cardinals, the highest-scoring team in 1942, were batting .204, last in the league, after the first week of the season.

As of April 29 the National League was hitting .238, down from the 1942 average of .249. The falloff in hitting in the American League was even more dramatic— .257 to .210. One player who refused to succumb to the plague of anemic hitting was Stan Musial. The Man, off on a characteristic spring tear, was hitting .333. But even his best shots were staying in the park. In truth, Musial's sharp line drives over the infielders were all that kept the Cardinals' team average from resembling a feverish man's body temperature.

How about the American League, you ask? The league of DiMaggio, Greenberg and Williams? Forget those guys. They were off to war. Want to know who was leading the circuit in home runs on April 29? The entire New York Yankee team, that's who. The team had one home run. The St. Louis Browns had one, also. The other six teams didn't have any. The goose egg was everywhere.

Subtly, game strategy in 1943 began to change. Baseball wisdom now called for a base runner to go for every conceivable inch if a batter happened to get a hit. The runner, it was assumed, might not see another hit as a young man. Consider a game between the Phillies and Dodgers in Shibe Park. Phillies shortstop Glen Stewart—who, in fine Phillies tradition, entered the game with a career. 138 average from the lively ball era—led off by poking a single past the bewildered infielders. Up came third baseman Pinky May. May had occasional power. Very occasional—three home runs over the past four seasons. O.K... light hitter...runner on first...sacrifice maybe?

The infielders crept in. So did the outfielders.

May slashed the ball to the power alley in left center. Stewart ran like the wind, around second, around third. He never stopped until he reached home plate, where Dodger catcher Mickey Owen was waiting for him with the balata. One out. But May, unaccustomed to luxury, never stopped running either. Owen threw the ball to Billy Herman, who was playing third. Herman tagged May. The Phillies had added a new dimension to baseball lore. Two batters, two hits and two outs. Never mind 'inside baseball.' Never mind Money Ball. Or Power Ball.

This was balata ball.

A few days into the season, a beleaguered Spalding vice-president responded to public criticism of the new ball. The balata was not to blame, he said. The culprit was some nasty cold weather, combined with unexpectedly fine pitching by previously mediocre hurlers. But within days, Spalding had taken a second look at its balata concoction and admitted that the first shipment of baseballs "did not measure up to standards." Corrections were hastily ordered at the factory, and Judge Landis renewed his request for a dose of jackrabbit in the updated version. The problems, Spalding assured baseball, would be solved.

Well, almost. The American League chose to continue to use the dead balls until May 9, when all eight parks were to receive the improved balls. Meanwhile, in several National League parks, hundreds of 1942 baseballs were still in storage; equipment managers had simply not yet returned them to Spalding, as was customary.

So out they came, setting off a new controversy: Could two different balls be used in one game? The rule book was scrutinized. There was apparently nothing against it. So the teams that had the '42 balls started slugging again, while the rest stayed mired in 1908-style baseball. In the first game in which the '42 ball was used, the Dodgers celebrated by thrashing the Phillies 11-4 at Ebbets Field. There were 23 hits. Across town, playing in a game that was entirely different, Spud Chandler of the Yankees came within one pitch of no-hitting the Senators. And so it went, though cynics noted that the Senators often had trouble hitting any kind of ball.

Two weeks into the season, National League president Ford Frick invited reporters to his New York office to introduce them to the "new" revised balata ball. This one substituted a synthetic rubber cement (which remained gummy and sticky) for the two hard balata shells within the ball. When dropped on the hardwood floor of Frick's office, the revised baseball drew smiles all around. It bounced twice as high as its predecessor, meaning it was almost half again as resilient as a 1942 baseball. Both leagues, delighted with the revision, agreed to begin using the balata again.

The National League didn't have enough of the good old 1942 baseballs to last the entire season anyway. When the balata was put into play in the American League that Sunday, batters teed off for six home runs. Previously there had been nine home runs in 72 games. Landis, who

147

was in Chicago at the time, was pleased, and said so. "I'm glad they've found out what's wrong. I think this will settle the whole matter."

As the season progressed, the controversy faded. The ball was revised and revised again until it became acceptably lively, although it was still not the jackrabbit Landis wanted. But 1943 continued to be a very quirky year. More than once in that season, visiting managers, watching hometown pitchers mow down their troops, wondered if a balata pelota had been smuggled into play. Occasionally one was, but the ball was also a handy excuse for a poor game. O'Neill, a man fated to be tortured by the dead ball, caught the Philadelphia A's tossing balatas at his club in Shibe Park on June 1. He protested the game, a loss in the nightcap of a doubleheader. But Harridge disallowed the protest after discovering that the dreaded "cement clunker"—as sportswriters called it—had surfaced in the first game, too, uncontested and unnoticed by the Tigers, who had won that one 7-0.

In the World Series the Cardinals played the Yankees, suggesting that whatever the makeup of the baseball, everyone had been victimized equally over the course of 154 games. In the end the best teams had won anyway.

Uncle Sam took the major leagues off the hook the following winter. By then synthetic rubber was being manufactured on a large scale in the U.S. and supplies were readily available. There was enough for tanks and airplanes and baseballs. Nineteen forty-four opened sunny and clear, with good, lively Spaldings in abundance. It was like the return of an old friend; hitting was back.

There was only one hitch, as someone noticed a few days into the season. There weren't that many good hardwood bats around. The wartime supply of wood and wood pulp was being diverted into more urgent uses, and, well...a good solid ash bat was suddenly damned hard to find. But professional athletes, like everyone else, had to learn to make do during war. And bats were an entirely different story.

*

Traditional cork centered baseball on left, balata ball on right.

(Courtesy: US Library of Congress.)

**"O'Malley wanted to move the Dodgers out
of Brooklyn because he saw the promised land. He was
right about that, but to this day I think he was wrong to
take the Dodgers out of Brooklyn."**

**Jerry Reinsdorf, who was born
in Brooklyn but owns the
Chicago Bulls and Chicago White Sox**

Chapter 12 - 2 BR, 1 BTH APT, UNDER LF GRANDSTAND, 155th STREET

By the autumn of 1945, Horace Stoneham, owner of the New York Giants baseball team, knew he had a serious problem—and it wasn't that his team had finished in the second division for the last three years. It was the ballpark. The Giants' home, the Polo Grounds, was a comfortable, historic old place where the great John J. McGraw had managed the Giants to ten pennants. It was where Babe Ruth had hit his first New York home runs. It was the arena where Red Grange had made his debut as a pro football player and where Jack Dempsey had knocked out Luis Firpo after Firpo had put Dempsey through the ropes.

But the playing area for baseball was ragged. Rumor had it that the grounds crews were spending more time on long, liquid lunches than on maintaining the field.

The situation was made all the more acute by Branch Rickey, president of the Brooklyn Dodgers. Whenever Stoneham and traveling secretary Eddie Brannick ventured to Ebbets Field, Rickey loved to crow about what great shape his own field was in.

After Rickey needled Stoneham one time too many, Horace went looking for help. His attention settled on Matthew Schwab Jr., one of the best groundskeepers in the business, if not *the* best. Matty's grandfather, John Schwab, had first gone into the craft at Redland Field in Cincinnati in 1883. And Matty's father, Matthew Sr., was still with the Cincinnati club in the same capacity. It was Matthew, Senior whom we saw in the rowboat with Lee Grissom.

As for Matty, well, he was the head groundskeeper at Ebbets Field. He was just what the Polo Grounds needed. So at the end of 1945, when Stoneham learned that Rickey, a legendarily tightfisted employer, had once again denied Matty a long-deserved, long-deferred raise, the Giants' owner sent Brannick to Schwab's winter home in Florida to ask Matty if he would care to come over to the Polo Grounds.

Schwab said yes. Rickey woke up not too many mornings later to discover that Stoneham had swiped his head groundskeeper and was taking him to upper Manhattan. In the never-ending war between the Giants and the Dodgers, it was a masterful shot.

Caring for the playing field of the Polo Grounds presented some unique problems. Permitting fans to amble across the field after a game didn't make the maintenance of the stadium any easier, but then there was the specific problem of the location. Stabilization needed to be done on the Polo Grounds field every fall and winter to minimize the natural sinking of the earth beneath the ballpark, something made even worse by the bustling rumbling subway line that ran beneath the adjacent parking area. In the mid-1940's, the Giants spent more than $125,000 to elevate the field and modernize the drainage. Needed: approximately 3,000 cubic yards of gravel, 1,500 cubic yards of topsoil, and 160,000 square feet of sod.

One unforeseen, problem soon developed, however.

Schwab lived with his wife, Rose, and four-year-old son, Jerry, in a nice apartment on President Street in Brooklyn. The commute by car to the Polo Grounds at 155th Street and 8th Avenue in Manhattan could be counted on for a couple of hours of torture every day. For a short time Schwab and his family moved into the Concourse Plaza Hotel near the ballpark.

Now, the Concourse Plaza Hotel was not exactly low-brow digs. It was a luxury hotel located at Grand Concourse and 161st Street in the Bronx, just across the Macomb's Dam Bridge – to be clear, that's *Macomb's* with a 'b' and *dam* without the 'n' - from Manhattan. The hotel was within easy walking distance of Yankee Stadium and not too distant from the Polo Grounds. The hotel opened in 1923. Babe Ruth stayed there during some homestands (or at least his suitcase did) and several decades later so did Mickey Mantle and Roger Maris of the Yankees and Frank Gifford of the Football Giants. Often American League visiting teams would stay there, too. In short, for years it was the best location in the Bronx for social, business and fraternal events. Tito Puente's band played in the grand ballroom every New Year's Eve for a dance that drew 1200 people. When Senator John F. Kennedy, the Democratic Party candidate for President arrived there in 1960, an impromptu friendly-as-chicken-soup sign greeted him with the words, "The home of the knishes thinks Jack is delicious." But times changed. Yankees second-baseman Horace Clarke was reportedly the last Yankees player to make the hotel his in-season residence during the 1960s and early 1970s.

Back in the late 1940's when the Schwab family stayed there it was an improvement on the car trek from Brooklyn, but less than perfect. Plus, let's face it, the Grand Concourse was Yankee territory and what family wants to live in a hotel, anyway?

{Author's note: At this writing in 2019, the building has long since closed as a hotel and is now a senior citizens residence owned and operated by the City of New York City.}

Yet there was no convenient, reasonable housing anywhere closer to the Polo Grounds. That's when Schwab noticed some unused space below the leftfield grandstand at the ballpark.

"I asked Mr. Stoneham whether it would be possible to build a place to live right there," explained Matty Schwab many years later from his home in Fort Lauderdale, Florida. "He said it was unheard of. But Mr. Stoneham always took care of his employees. So he asked Joe Traynor, the park superintendent, to see what could be done."

153

Soon carpenters were at work under the grandstand, followed by electricians and plumbers. Eventually there emerged a cozy two-bedroom apartment with bath, kitchen and living room, plus a private entrance and free parking. By 1946, the new digs were ready for a move-in. The year was unsuccessful on the field for the Giants. Raided by the Mexican League, the club finished in eighth place. At the turnstiles, the story was different. The turnstiles buzzed in baseball-crazy postwar New York City: the Giants drew 1,219,873 paying customers, a new franchise record. And unbeknownst to almost all of the fans who pushed through the Polo Grounds turnstiles, the Schwab family had taken up residence at the ballpark, just beyond the outfield fence.

"The foul line," recalled Schwab, "was on the other side of my living room wall. Bobby Thomson's home run, the one that won us the pennant in 1951, landed on my roof."

There were windows on three sides of the apartment; two faced some subway repair yards across the street from the park and another looked out on an alley. Soon Matty began to dream about a fourth exposure.

"I asked," he said with a sly chuckle, "if I could put in another window. You know, in the outfield wall facing the field. But Mr. Stoneham finally said no."

Only Rose had the slightest complaint: The place did get a little noisy from time to time, particularly during boisterous doubleheaders when the Dodgers were visiting. Imagine a party going on in an upstairs apartment with 56,000 people in attendance, half of whom hate the other half, and you get the idea.

There was no direct access from the outside to the apartment. The family had to come and go through one of the roll-up metal gates that led to the outside. More usually, however, they would come and go by auto, driving through the concourse under the stands and emerging from a gate in right center field onto Eighth Avenue in Manhattan.

Schwab may have been partway to paradise, but his son was already there. "The biggest backyard in Manhattan," Matty used to call the playing field. On warm summer nights, Jerry, an eight-year-old in 1950, would invite friends over, pitch a tent and camp out beneath the stars. The grassy turf that Sid Gordon and Thomson—and later Hall of Famers Monte Irvin and Willie Mays—roamed by daylight was Jerry's private playground for countless nights.

Even years later those boyhood memories remained vivid. "On some nights when I didn't camp out, I would get up every two hours to help my father move the sprinklers around the field," said Jerry, who grew up to be he branch manager of a post office in Fort Lauderdale.

"My father used to send me into the dugouts sometimes to turn hoses on or off. It was pitch black. I never knew what monsters might be waiting in the darkness." He laughed. "But none ever were."

Daylight brought the ball players, arriving for work around ten a.m. for a day game. "There were three of us kids who were tolerated by the players," remembered Jerry, "though I was the only one who actually lived there. Me, Chris [son of Giant skipper Leo] Durocher and Dale [son of star pitcher Larry] Jansen. We wore New York Giants uniforms, just like the batboys. We had the run of the park. If we wanted to go somewhere we'd take one of the many underground tunnels and pop out of a manhole. We'd stand behind the batting cage and watch the pitchers. Then we'd work out with the players and shag flies in the outfield. There was only one place we knew not to go: the clubhouse after Durocher had slammed the door. That meant he was about to yell at his players."

The kids had a Little League team – mostly sons of Giants players and employees - that used the field when the team was away. They would also race around the stands and concourses on bikes when the Giants were out of town.

Jerry was particularly close to pitcher Jim Hearn, but it was slugger Johnny Mize who was his boyhood hero. "I wore number 15 on my uniform, same as Mize, before they sold him to the Yankees. After he left, I still kept his number."

Then there were the retired Hall of Famers who used to pass by: Mel Ott, Bill Terry, Carl Hubbell. Mays arrived in 1951 as a frightened kid. Then in 1952 there came a 28-year-old rookie with an unorthodox pitch, Hoyt Wilhelm. Wilhelm, the future Hall of Famer, and Jerry took a liking to each other.

"Hoyt made me a whiz on my high school baseball team," Jerry recalled. "He taught me how to throw a knuckleball."

As the condition of the playing field improved under Schwab's scrupulous care, so did the Giants under Durocher. There was the miracle pennant in 1951, then the heady World Championship in 1954, which featured The Catch by Willie Mays off Vic Wertz and Dusty Rhodes' timely pinch hitting. Never mind that Wertz's 475 foot blast was an out and Rhodes' 280 foot pop up was a home run. As Casey Stengel used to ask, "What would you rather be good or lucky.

Schwab received a full share of the World Series money that year, plus a Series ring. But by then the team was starting to unravel. Durocher quit. Irvin, Thomson, Al Dark and Whitey Lockman were all traded. Bummer!

At the same time, the neighborhood began to change, and the concrete-and-steel structure of the Polo Grounds, erected in 1911, began to creak. Inevitably, talk centered on sites for a new ballpark in New York. It all must have been terribly unsettling for the Schwab family. It was their home that people wanted to abandon.

"It would be hard to take if the Giants ever moved to another park," Matty Schwab commented in 1956. "Even

156

if I found a place to live right across the street, I'd still feel like a commuter."

With no new park forthcoming in New York, Stoneham sent Schwab, among others, west to scout prospective playing fields, such as Minneapolis. Meanwhile, the Mayor of San Francisco and Walter O'Malley were whispering enticements into Horace Stoneham's ears. When the Giants did decide on another place to live, it was across the continent in San Francisco.

On Sept. 29, 1957, the last Giants home game was played in the old park. And the end, as Schwab had predicted, was hard to take. "I guess I'm dispossessed," Matty said as the gates finally clanked shut.

The Schwabs went west with the team. Matty presided at Seals Stadium, then at Candlestick, although he couldn't really call either of them home. Jerry, a young man by this time, worked with the grounds crew before moving on to other things. Matty remained with the Giants until 1979, long enough to see Jerry's son become a bat-boy, the fifth generation of Schwabs to work on a big league ball field.

"I'm sorry I never went back to the Polo Grounds as an adult," Jerry remembered years later. "I would have liked to see it through the eyes of a grownup and compare it to my memories as a boy. But I never got back there. It bothers me."

Demolition crews struck first, knocking down the old park in November 1964. With it went the Schwabs' apartment, which was used for groundskeeping equipment during the Met's tenure there in 1962 and 1963, but never again as New York City's most unique residence.

An Ebbets Field Reminiscence

Ebbets Field was not a pitcher's park. There was very little foul territory. The distance down the right field line was 297 feet. The scoreboard was 318. You had to pitch very well to win a game there. I didn't make changes in the way I pitched from park to park. We were an offensive club. I just tried to go to the mound with my best stuff. My goal was to hold the other side for one more inning.

I was the player representative in 1956. (General Manager) Buzzie Bavasi came to me one day and said the Dodgers had a chance to get Sal Maglie from Cleveland. I asked, "Is he healthy?" (Maglie, the one-time fierce adversary and former New York Giant, had had a bad back.) Buzzie said he was healthy but he was wondering about the reception Maglie would get from the Dodgers. "Well, he better have a bodyguard in the clubhouse," I said. "But if he's healthy, get him."

I admired Maglie. He was always competitive and in control on the mound. We got him. The first time he walked into the locker room, Carl Furillo (with whom Maglie had had some high profile feuds on the field) looks at him and says, "Hey, Paesan'." Sal pitched well for us. (13-5, 2.71) There was the no hitter in September plus the World Series. He pitched well against Larsen in the perfect game.

My best memories? The 14 Strikeouts in the (1953) World Series. The World Championships in 1955. The two no hitters (1952 vs. Chicago and 1956 vs. New York Giants.) Ten years of pitching in Brooklyn. It was great.

Carl Erskine
Anderson, Indiana
June 2019

{Author's note: Carl Erskine was the mainstay of the Brooklyn Dodger pitching staffs in the final era at Ebbets Field. He was 20-6 in 1953. He won 118 games as a Brooklyn Dodger (out of a career total of 122) and ranks 5th in career wins behind Dazzy Vance, Burleigh Grimes, Nap Rucker and Don Newcombe in the modern era of the Brooklyn Dodgers. Signed photo from the author's personal collection.}

An Ebbets Field Reminiscence

I first met Carl Erskine in 2013 when he visited the fire station and had breakfast with us. We cooked him biscuits and gravy. The movie *42* was about to premier so we thought it would be great to have him up to talk about the movie. He spent a couple hours with us. Six years later we are very close friends and I see him every week and talk to him at least twice a week. That's how our friendship started. We got real close when I became (his son) Jimmy's bowling coach with the Special Olympics.

The other day, "Oisk" had me over to look at some baseball cards someone gave him and he had a photo for me. Carl came across the original photo in some things he had put up. Stan Musial and Carl played against each other for many years in the National League. Carl said Stan had 167 at bats and a little over 70 hits against him (.419). Stan was Carl's toughest hitter. It gave Carl great pleasure to say that Stan only hit 4 home runs and only struck out 4 times against Oisk. Stan Musial hit 475 home runs in his career. For years Stan said he spent his whole career trying to figure out how to hit Carl and Carl says he spent his career trying to figure out how to strike Stan out.

The two loved to play the harmonica and actually played together in St Louis one evening. Carl has a song that he does in his harmonica. It's my favorite one and he calls it *The Stan Musial Blues*. It refers to how tough Musial was to get out at the plate.

What a photo this is! I must've thanked him 10 times!

Jim Denny
Anderson, Indiana
May 2019

{Photo courtesy of Jim Denny, from his personal collection.}

*

"Brooklyn was a lovely place to hit. If you got a ball in the air, you had a chance to get it out. When they tore down Ebbets Field, we wept. They tore down a little piece of me."

Duke Snider

*

"The catch off Bobby Morgan (a running backhanded catch of a line drive in September 1951 at Ebbets Field) in Brooklyn was the best catch I ever made. Jackie Robinson and Leo Durocher were the first people I saw when I opened my eyes."

Willie Mays

Babe Ruth – Brooklyn Dodger Coach and Bobblehead

Among the many definitions for the word "Ruthless" might be "the New York Yankees after 1934." The Babe left the Bronx in that year after 15 seasons. But he wasn't completely finished with baseball. Ruth bounced back to Boston – where his major league career had begun - to play with the Braves for 28 games and 6 home runs. The more telling numbers, however, were his age, 40, and batting average, .181 in 1935. Maybe it ain't over till it's over but in this case it was emphatically over.

Ruth wanted to manage the Yankees. That wasn't going to happen.

Most people in Yankee management who had any input were of the opinion that Ruth couldn't manage himself, much less a team. Assessing the situation, and not receiving any offers from the New York Giants, and obviously not wanting to give up his luxury digs on Riverside Drive in Manhattan, the Babe settled upon the third team in town, the Dodgers, who were frequently having attendance problems and hadn't won a pennant since 1920.

So George Herman Ruth passed the 1938 season as the first base coach with the Brooklyn Dodgers. How out of place did he look in a Dodger uniform? Very. And the relationship wasn't terribly warm. According to observers within the Dodger clubhouse at the time, The Bambino wasn't even allowed to relay the signs to baserunners, those came from the bench, which meant Burleigh Grimes, the spitball pitcher turned manager. Ruth was also informed in no uncertain terms that he would not be considered to manage the club when the position became available, which in those days it frequently did.

The Babe's real function was to burnish the
Dodgers daffy image in that era and to take batting practice
with the team. Ruth may have had an expansive gut by age
forty and the legs were brittle and gone. But he could still
swing a bat, amuse the fans who got there early, and drop a
few balls out onto Bedford Avenue.

It was an easy job, but not much to Ruth's liking.
The Dodgers lurched to a seventh place finish, then
compounded the 'insult' to Ruth by firing Burleigh Grimes,
the manager for two years, and hiring Ruth's nasty little
nemesis, Leo Durocher.

It was not a happy time for Mr. Ruth. There are
many pictures of him in a Brooklyn uniform. In most of
them, he is not smiling.

If hiring Ruth as a promotion was odd enough in 1938, the Los Angeles Dodgers took it one better in 2013 by announcing the Babe would be back in uniform…as a bobblehead.

That is correct. The former star with the Yankees and the Red Sox would be a bobblehead to be given away on September 9, 2013, the date of a game against the San Diego Padres. A few years later, the Atlanta Braves offered a similar item, Ruth as a Boston Brave.

This conjured up a whole new world of possible promotions: the Elston Howard and Tom Seaver Red Sox bobbleheads, the Reggie Jackson Baltimore Oriole bobblehead, Steve Carlton of the Twins, Warren Spahn of the Mets and so on.

The first base coaching job was actually Ruth's last job in baseball until the next century. One wonders if somewhere in the afterlife, the Babe is having a cold beer, a cigar and a good laugh. We see him here in his final uniform as a player or coach, looking toward Heaven.

.

Chapter 13 - The Most Famous Brooklyn Dodger You've Never Heard Of

Otto Miller was the catcher when Brooklyn hurler Nap Rucker threw the first pitch at Ebbets Field in 1913. Miller also had two of the Brooklyn team's six hits that day. As noted earlier, Miller was also there when the curtain came down on the team at Ebbets Field in 1957.

He played thirteen seasons (1910-1922) for Brooklyn under two managers, Bill Dahlen and Wilbert Robinson and was later a coach for eleven years under three skippers, Robinson, Max Carey and Casey Stengel.

Otto Miller should be an icon of Brooklyn baseball. Instead, he has almost vanished into history. Even Peter Golenbock's wonderful book, *Bums*, never mentions him. Oy vey. What a shame! The man played his entire career in a Brooklyn uniform and caught for more seasons than anyone, even Roy Campanella.

So let's shine some light on his memory.

Miller was born in Nebraska on June 1, 1889. He was nicknamed, "Moonie," probably because big guys who had round friendly faces in those days were frequently called just that. Moonie batted and threw right-handed. When he played ball, he was listed at an even six feet and weighed nearly 200 pounds. He was "a big fella," as Vin Scully might have said, particularly for the day. His given name was "Lowell Otto" but he always chose to reverse the first two names and be known as "Otto." His family name was actually Mueller. So Lowell Otto Mueller over the years became Otto Miller.

Miller joined Brooklyn in 1910, having spent time in the minor leagues at Sharon of the Ohio-Pennsylvania League and Duluth of the Minnesota-Wisconsin League. At the time, "Bad" Bill Dahlen was the manager and Tex

167

Erwin and Bill Bergen were the regular catchers. The team was known as the Superbas, named after a vaudeville troupe. The team was popular in the borough but was a couple of decades away from being officially known as the Dodgers.

Otto didn't get into a game until July 16 of that same year when he relieved Erwin behind the plate during the second game of a double header against the Cardinals at Robison Field in St. Louis, the predecessor of Sportsman's Park. By a strange coincidence, a young pitcher named Fred "Speedy" Miller came in to pitch at the same time. The arrival of the two Millers gave Brooklyn their only Miller-Miller battery ever. (Fred Miller would be 1-1 in 6 games for Brooklyn that year, then quickly vanish from the major leagues.)

As a hitter, Otto did not impress. But as a defensive catcher, he was as good as anyone of his era. Otto got into 27 more games that year, remained with Brooklyn as a back-up catcher in 1911 and then became the hard working regular in 1912, a year when Nap Rucker was the mainstay of the Brooklyn staff, winning 22 games. He hit with no power and had an average that usually hovered around .220. But his mechanics behind the plate were excellent. He handled pitchers extremely well.

Remember Bill Bergen, one of the catchers who was ahead of Miller on the team? Despite the fact that Miller was never much of a hitter, Bergen was even less of one. Bergen was perhaps one of the finest defensive catchers to ever play. Unfortunately, no one – *no one!* - played in the major leagues as long as Bill Bergen and hit with such a low average. Bergen had 3,028 career at-bats, during which he astonished people with hits 516 times and compiled a career batting average of .170. So after 1911, Bergen was gone and Otto Miller became the starting catcher, at least for a time. Bergen is still a favorite of "stat heads," however, with his lowest batting average of all

168

time. The great Cy Young, a contemporary, had a higher
career batting average: .210

These were not yet glory days for the Brooklyn
team. Brooklyn had won National League pennants in 1889
and 1890 but had plunged back into gritty mediocrity in the
mid 1890's. Then there had been a renaissance when Ned
Hanlon took control of the franchise and brought with him
from Baltimore the nucleus of a fine club. Brooklyn again
topped the National League in 1899 and 1900. Then
Hanlon left and darkness descended again.

In the first years of the new century, Charles Ebbets
acquired majority ownership of the team. The Superbas
played in Washington Park at Fifth Avenue and Third
Street in Brooklyn. Ebbets began to quietly acquire land for
a new ballpark With the land secured, Ebbets put half a
million dollars into a construction project "on the outskirts
of Flatbush." There, in a fetid swampy area that had once
been called "Pigtown," Ebbets Field would rise.

At the same time, Ebbets started putting together a
competitive ball club. In Zack Wheat and Jake Daubert he
had two of the best players in the league. New players lifted
the club past their absolutely miserable 1912 season when
the club finished last with a winning percentage of .370. In
Nap Rucker and Sherry Smith, they had two solid starters
to anchor their pitching staff. In Miller, they had a fine
defensive catcher in what was then a defensive position in
baseball. In right field they had Casey Stengel who, many
people forget, was a fine player in his day in addition to
just being Casey Stengel.

Ebbets also had a major annoyance. It was called
the Federal League, a third major league that put eight
teams in the field in 1914 and 1915, driving up players'
salaries and owners' costs. There was a team in Brooklyn
called the Tip Tops, owned by Robert Ward, a wealthy
baker who baked Tip Top Bread. The Tip Tops played in

Washington Park, which the Brooklyn Nationals had abandoned after 1912 for Charlie Ebbets' new field.

By now Miller was in his early 20's, a big powerfully built catcher and a very popular guy with the fans. The Federal League owners coveted many of Ebbets' players, Wheat, Daubert and Miller in particular. Charlie had a solution to that problem. He wanted his players, too. So he paid them. Miller received a three year contract. He celebrated by marrying a Brooklyn girl named Madeline Dowe in 1915.

In true Brooklyn fashion, memorable events had their way of finding Miller.

That same spring of 1915 in Daytona Beach, aviator Ruth Law had been throwing golf balls out of her airplane as a publicity stunt to boost a local golf course. At some point, someone suggested throwing a baseball from her airplane. Brooklyn manager Wilbert Robinson, who had taken over the club in 1913, agreed to try to catch the baseball. Law flew her plane approximately 525 feet above Robinson. However, Law realized she had forgotten her baseball and threw a grapefruit that she had with her. When Robinson tried to catch it, the grapefruit hit his glove and exploded in his face. Miller and Casey Stengel were among the amused witnesses.

In 1916, Robinson guided the Brooklyns to their first National League pennant in the modern era. Other National League teams were weakened by raids from the Federal League and Brooklyn, where Ebbets had paid to keep his best players, took advantage. Chief Meyers came over to Brooklyn from the Giants, as did Rube Marquard. Meyers and Miller shared the catching during the season. Meyers did most of the catching in the World Series against the Red Sox but Miller was in two games.

Game Two of the World Series was a classic.

170

Miller collected one of 6 hits against Babe Ruth, who pitched all 14 innings in a legendary 2-1 Boston win in front of more than forty thousand fans at Braves Field. Sherry Smith, the Dodger hurler whom Miller caught, pitched the game of his life, but still was on the short end of the decision. (Smith is at left in the photo here from the 1916 World Series, Otto Miller is at right.) Gate attendance was the primary revenue for a club in that era, hence the larger stadium in  Boston was used instead of Fenway. Boston went on to win the World Series. In a strange quirk of baseball fate, the two franchises would not meet again in the postseason for 102 years, many years after the Dodgers had relocated to Los Angeles. The record for most innings played in a World Series game, fourteen, remained from 1916. It was broken in Game 3 in 2018 when the same two franchises played eighteen innings. And once again, the Boston team would eventually go on to defeat the Dodgers.

Four years later, Miller again would be at the center of a piece of baseball history.

Miller had his best season at the plate in 1920, hitting .289. Brooklyn won the National League pennant. Zack Wheat was still on the team, and so was Nap Rucker, two of the great players of Brooklyn baseball in the first third of the Twentieth Century. So was Burleigh Grimes, the great spitball pitcher, whom Miller often caught.

The Cleveland Indians awaited in the World Series.

In the fifth inning of Game Five of the 1920 World Series, played at League Park in Cleveland, Pete Kilduff, the Brooklyn second baseman, singled to lead off the inning. Otto Miller followed with another single. That brought up pitcher Clarence Mitchell in what might have been a sacrifice situation.

But Mitchell was a good hitting pitcher. He had hit .234 that year and .367 the previous season. Manager Wilbert Robinson occasionally used him at first base or in the corner outfield positions. So Mitchell wasn't bunting. Instead, he hit one of the most famous line drives in baseball history.

Well, the line drive wasn't so famous, but what happened to it was.

Second baseman Bill Wambsganss of Cleveland caught the line drive. He stepped on second base to retire Pete Kilduff, and then tagged an astonished Otto Miller coming from first base. One, two, three. It happened so fast that it was over within ten seconds, completing the first, and to date, *only* unassisted triple play in World Series history. It could only happen in Brooklyn....or to a team from Brooklyn.

Otto Miller's career as a backstop in Brooklyn lasted 937 games and more than three thousand plate appearances over 13 years. Roy Campanella caught more games, had more plate appearances and was far superior in every offensive category. But no one caught for more years at Ebbets Field. Miller caught thirteen. Campy caught ten.

Miller left the Brooklyn roster after the 1922 season, but not the organization. The Robins had a working agreement with Atlanta in the Sally League. Miller went there as a playing manager in 1923, catching 103 games. The next year, 1924, he went to Indianapolis of the American Association where he served as a coach but also caught in 43 games, hitting .377.

In 1925, he moved back to Brooklyn and bought a house at 1399 East 21st Street. He had a young family –

eventually he had two sons and a daughter and chose to raise them in Brooklyn. He was between jobs in the major leagues or high minors, so he made a living catching for semi-pro and amateur clubs, mostly around the borough, including the legendary Brooklyn Bushwicks. The Bushwicks were an independent, semi-professional baseball team that played in Dexter Park in Queens from 1913 to 1951. Dexter Park was located in Woodhaven, Queens, just north of Eldert Lane and Jamaica Avenue, not far from the borough line with Brooklyn.

Late in the 1925 season, Otto dropped by Ebbets Field one afternoon to watch a game. Uncle Robbie spotted him in the box seats. A conversation ensued and Robinson signed Otto as a coach for the 1926 season. He worked with Robbie's catchers and pitchers and became Robbie's "first lieutenant" according to The New York *Times* in 1927.

Robinson was fired at the end of the 1931 season, but by this time Miller had become a popular fixture at Ebbets Field, as well as a guy who loved to chat with fans. Max Carey followed Robinson for 1932 and 1933. Then Casey Stengel, Miller's former teammate, was hired as a manager.

Miller became Stengel's first base coach and stayed with the club until 1936, completing 24 years with the team. Dispensing baseball advise and wisdom was a big part of his role on the Brooklyn club as the years went by. He was seen on the club as a big brother or wise uncle to many young players as well as a buffer between young players and the manager.

Said differently, Miller was "a helpful soft-soaper to smooth ruffled feelings" of a player bawled out by the skipper, said *The Sporting News* in 1936. He occupied the role that Jake Pitler occupied in later years.

He was a man of "tolerant good nature," the publication said. "Otto goes on and on," the paper said, "like Tennyson's rippling brook," referencing the refrain from *The Brook*, the poem by Alfred Lord Tennyson: "For men may come and men may go, But I go on forever."

Miller was also bemused by Stengel's efforts to win with a motley cast of players in the mid 1930's. "(Casey reminds me) of a guy who has made up his mind to force a pair of deuces to beat four aces," he remarked at the time, "but can't give up trying."

Miller left the Dodgers after the 1936 season, but never left Brooklyn. He took jobs managing bars and owned a tavern. He was never far from Ebbets Field, either physically or in spirit.

"Otto Miller had sufficient exposure and personal contact to qualify as one of the best known Dodger heroes," commented columnist Jimmy Powers of the New York *Daily News* in the early 1960s. Ordinary fans would come by his bar just to have a beer, talk baseball with him, have another beer, ask his opinion on players, have a few more beers and get an autograph. He had a tremendous following in the borough. He was invited to weddings and wakes, picnics and christenings. He went to hundreds of events, if not thousands, and was a living link to the Brooklyn squads of the Twenties and Thirties, the time before the era of Durocher or Campanella or Robinson or Hodges.

He was a favorite of New York sportswriters, who sought his opinion. "A wonderful gregarious soul," said Powers, who knew Miller as a friend for decades.

Those who knew Otto Miller knew how he loved to tell of Wilbert Robinson's days as an Oriole in the 1890's. Miller must have recounted more than a thousand times how Uncle Robbie as a young man once hit safely seven straight times. Or how he broke a finger during a game, stuck it in mud for a minute to "cure" it, then continued catching. The team was known as the "Robins" in the Robinson era. Miller had unwavering affection and respect for his old manager.

"He was a kindly and gentle man," Miller recalled whenever Robbie's name would come up. "He got more out of his boys than any other man could. His boys played their hearts out for him because they loved him."

Miller also liked to reference that triple play in the World Series.

"Poor Clarence Mitchell," he used to say with a laugh. "The next time up after the triple play, he hit into a double play. He must be the only guy who hit into five outs in two at bats."

Otto Miller died in Brooklyn at the age of 72. It would have been nice if he could have left this world gently, but that was not the case. Miller had cataract surgery on his left eye on March 29, 1962, at the Brooklyn Eye and Ear Hospital at 29 Greene Street. Sometime following his operation, Miller was left unattended, wandered around the ward and somehow fell through a screen on a fourth floor window. He plunged to his death, landing on the Cumberland Street side of the hospital. The New York *Times* carried a prominent obituary, referring to Otto as "the Dodgers' old catcher and coach." The borough mourned. Otto was buried upstate in Goshen, New York

"Otto was a living link to the past," wrote a deeply saddened Jimmy Powers the next day. "His passing reminds us that his type of player is no longer with us."

A significant link to the Brooklyn Dodgers of the early Twentieth Century also disappeared with Otto Miller. How many others, for example, were there at Ebbets the day the park opened and the day it closed?

Already in 1962, there was an expansion New York team in the National League called The Mets. They were managed by Otto's old former teammate and manager in Brooklyn, Casey Stengel, wore Dodger blue and had a few old Dodgers on the roster. But the transplanted Dodgers themselves had taken root far away in Los Angeles where the stars were now named Koufax and Drysdale, Wills and Davis. It wasn't quite the same, but there was no reason in the world that it ever could have been.

Now Comes Miller Time!

As befits a player of Otto Miller's long popularity, many baseball cards bore his likeness. Some are more than a hundred years old. Others are shockingly current. Here are a few from the author's collection.

Miller's likeness was on a card issued by the Cracker Jack company in 1915.

A midwestern clothing company named Burgess-Nash also included him on their cards in 1916, though Gimbel's in New York had a similar card. The cards were colorful for a while, then turned austere, almost severe, in 1917, with a war raging in Europe and all American men ordered to report to register for a draft  lottery after the United States entered the conflict in March of 1917. Notice the inexplicably similar poses in these two cards.

Perhaps the most unusual item by modern standards was Miller's inclusion on the 1914 B18 Baseball Blankets set. These items weren't cards at all. The set consisted of 91 unnumbered cloth squares that were originally issued as flannel inserts with different cigarette brands. They were made of a felt-like

material which held the cancer sticks in the pack. Many people liked to fashion the squares into quilts or blankets. Hence the name of the collection. Miller was one of the stars of the day included, along with Ty Cobb, Nap Rucker and Honus Wagner.

There was also a 1912 card which simply says, "Miller – Brooklyn - Nat." It was recently reprinted by The Lantern Press in Seattle and has been adapted as a baseball wall décor item. After all these years, Otto is still with us in some small way. You can find him at Walmart among other retailers.

Otto at Walmart in 2019? Who knew?

Chapter 14

Closing Time. The Final Mad Dash at The Polo Grounds

September 29, 1957 was a sunny humid afternoon in upper Manhattan.

Five days after the Dodgers had played their last game at Ebbets Field, the New York Giants hosted their own last home game at the rambling old stadium known as The Polo Grounds. Now the old place was an aging green ballpark able to seat fifty-five thousand. Once it had been a horse-shoe shaped wooden grandstand with a carriage drive that enclosed the outfield. Yet, it seemed so recently that Dusty Rhodes had tortured the Cleveland Indians in the 1954 World Series, or that Bobby Thomson had lined a home run into the lower stands in left field to cap the greatest pennant race of all time.

All of the past screamed out and seemed so recent. But it was all gone and what was happening seemed to be plain wrong, just as it was the previous Tuesday in Brooklyn with this same Pirates team. The Bucs seemed to be making an obnoxious habit of this.

On the right field grandstand there was a banner. "STAY TEAM STAY!" it begged. That same morning, head groundskeeper Matty Schwab had loaded a square of the center-field sod into a box for shipment to San Francisco. Photographers recorded the moment. The camera brigade also found Bobby Thomson, who had returned to the Giants mid-season in a trade. They posed him pointing to the spot in left-field where he had hit the most famous home run in baseball history. Thomson was a modest man who never would have stood there and pointed. But the camera guys posed him anyway. It was that sort of day.

Johnny Antonelli would pitch. Bobby Thomson was in the line-up at third base. Whitey Lockman had returned also. He was at first. For old times' sake, the final manager of the New York Giants, Bill Rigney, who had once been a deft infielder for the club, had placed the final links to recent glory in the starting lineup. Dusty Rhodes started, too, as did Willie Mays and Wes Westrum. But the sad truth was that the New York Giants were once again mired in sixth place, a position they had occupied a good deal of the time for the past three seasons.

Fewer than twelve thousand fans attended, proving something that Horace Stoneham had been insinuating: people weren't coming to the ballpark. In response, Horace was taking his fabled team to San Francisco.

It was unbelievable. New York's oldest team was leaving for a new life and new existence three thousand miles away. After eight decades of baseball at a place known as the Polo Grounds, there would be no baseball here the following April. For the New York Giants, winter would be forever.

Do you believe in ghosts? A few were on hand that day. You could have seen them in the Giants' locker room before the game. Now they were on the field as Russ

Hodges, the affable television and radio commentator for the team these last few years, conducted a ceremony drenched in sadness.

Rube Marquard, the star pitcher of the pre-World War One era was there, visiting the players, taking a last glance at the old park. He looked to be in good health, despite his sixty-eight years. His face was weathered, but he was lean and erect. Rube told a few of the vintage stories, like the way McGraw had paid eleven thousand bucks for him, only to watch him get shelled in his first outing. He was joined by George Burns, McGraw's left fielder from the World War I era. When Russ Hodges introduced them, older fans remembered and gave them applause.

Larry Doyle was there, too. He was no longer young and no longer a Giant, except in his heart, where he was both. He talked about coming to the club in 1904. McGraw took him out for a beer and Doyle was too scared to order anything but ginger ale.

Moose McCormick, who had played against the Red Sox and A's in the World Series of 1912 and 1913, was there, too. So was Rosy Ryan, who had struck out the great Babe Ruth more than a few times in the World Series in the 1920's. Carl Hubbell attended also, as did Mrs. Blanche McGraw, John's widow. Mrs. Jane Mathewson, Christy's widow, was invited but declined to attend. She said it would be too painful.

Many of the fans who showed up had been following the Giants since the turn of the century. In the poignant pre-game ceremony, they were happy to once again see Jack Doyle, Hook Wiltse, and other heroes of a bygone era. Jack Doyle, at age 86, was the oldest living ex-Giant. No relation to Larry, he was a native of Ireland who had played first base in the 1890s and managed in 1895. There also were Rosy Ryan, George (Kiddo) Davis, George Burns, Hans Lobert, Red Murray, Frank Frisch, and Moose

McCormick, players who went back many decades. They
had all played for John McGraw in the first third of the
Twentieth Century.

Hal Schumacher, Carl Hubbell, Blondie Ryan, Billy
Jurges, Buddy Kerr, Babe Young, Willard Marshall and Sid
Gordon were there, too. They were from the Bill Terry era.

Finally, from Leo Durocher's two pennant winning
clubs, there were Sal Maglie, Monte Irvin and Hank
Thompson, in addition to Mays, Bobby Thomson and
Rhodes who were still active. The loudest applause was for
pitchers Hubbell and Maglie, a lefty and a righty.

Maglie had gone on to play for other teams, including
the cross-borough Yankees and Dodgers. Today, all was
forgiven.

"If you had one game you had to win," said one fan,
"you'd want Maglie on the mound."

No one disagreed.

The sense of loss and the specters of the past were
painful. Carl Hubbell couldn't bear to think what might
become of the Polo Grounds. "I'd feel mighty bad to come
back here and see a housing project," he said. "New York
without the Giants just won't be the same."

Larry Doyle commented, "If you had told me a year
ago that they would be going to San Francisco, I would
have thought you were crazy."

Eddie Brannick, the Giants' long-time secretary who
had worked for the team for more than fifty years,
concurred. "It's a sad day. From 1905 is a long time," he
added. "But, like the song, I guess it's best just to say, 'Que
Sera Sera, whatever will be, will be.'"

Before the game, Bill Rigney walked around the
center field clubhouse, constantly singing *Bon Voyage*." He
said he couldn't keep it out of his head.

"I guess I'm a little nostalgic," Rigney said. "I'm
going to miss this place. I like San Francisco, but this place
here was our big goal when we were kids. Coming up

through the minors, we were just hoping to get to the Polo Grounds. Now we're leaving it."

Russ Hodges valiantly continued the ceremony at home plate. At that time, the fans in attendance had their chance to transmit their sentiments to Horace Stoneham, the owner who was moving the team. The fans, who felt as if they had been disowned, reacted predictably at the one mention of the club owner's name in pre-game ceremonies.

"Mr. Stoneham," said Hodges to an avalanche of long loud boos, "asked me to express his thanks for your being here with him and the Giants today." Hodges continued. "He wishes to thank you for your generous support through the years." He was greeted with an even louder chorus of derisive laughter, inventive profanity and more boos. "All the Giants will remember," Hodges finished.

The club owner was on the other side of a closed window in his upstairs office in the clubhouse, far from his customers.

One by one, as Hodges presided near home plate, every old-timer stepped up for his special moment. Hodges gave each a laminated picture of the Polo Grounds. The picture had been taken at least a decade earlier when there still were elevated tracks where the housing project now was, adjacent to the Giants' home.

Present but not introduced were Baseball Commissioner Ford Frick and National League President Warren Giles. To more than a few fans, they looked like honorary undertakers. Even Coogan's Bluff in the background looked forlorn.

Bill Rigney placed an arm of comfort around Mrs. Blanche McGraw, John's widow for more than two decades. When Rigney kissed Mrs. McGraw, for the benefit of the newsreels, she shed so many tears that someone had to find a handkerchief. Rigney later presented her a bouquet of American Beauty roses, per the day's script. Mrs. McGraw was challenged to smile.

"I still can't believe I'll never see the Polo Grounds again," she said. "New York can never be the same for me."

The Giants even brought back one of the original voices of the Polo Grounds, a gentleman named George Levy, now eighty-one. He announced the day's batteries through a megaphone, exactly as he had done it 50 years ago, before the advent of public address systems. He had the old megaphone with him today and made the final call, walking the aisles as he had done decades earlier, booming it out for all the ages and to all the corners of the grand old ballpark.

"The baaaaattttereeeees for today's gaaaaaaaame...."

The ceremony ended. But along with the move of the Dodgers to Los Angeles, which would not be "official" for another two weeks, nothing would ever be the same. The Giants and The Polo Grounds had once been the most famous names in baseball.

But not anymore.

Yes, a game of baseball would be played that day. But at the same moment something vital was being ripped out of the heart and soul of New York City.

The managers, Bill Rigney of the Giants and Danny Murtaugh of the Pittsburgh Pirates, met at home plate for the cursory mention of ground rules. They exchanged the starting line-ups. The umpires were Vic Delmore at home plate, Augie Donatelli at first, Vinnie Smith at second and Ed Sudol at third.

Johnny Antonelli (12-17) would pitch for the New York Giants. Bob Friend (13-18) would be on the mound for the Pirates. By a strange quirk of fate, the Giants would end New York's oldest baseball dynasty as they had begun it under Coogan's Bluff seven decades earlier, on July 8, 1889, when they had beaten the Pirates on this same field. What was it about the Pittsburgh club, opening and closing ball parks in New York?

At a few minutes after two p.m., the New York Giants took the field for the final time.

The game began. Antonelli gave up a single to Gene Freese in the top of the first, then a triple to Bob Skinner. Willie Mays, much in his prime, retrieved the ball and threw to the plate, nailing Skinner who had tried for an inside the park home run.

Then, for a few minutes, some of the old Giants magic was back in the bottom of the first.

Don Mueller singled with one out. Mays followed with a single, sending Mueller to third.

Dusty Rhodes batted and lofted a short fly to the outfield. Mueller broke for home and scored on a close play at the plate, evading a tag by a rookie catcher.

The Giants were tied 1-1 after one inning.

For a final time, the Giants fans settled into a game. The Pirates came to bat in the second inning.

It was difficult to fathom that this game was the end of the Giants in New York. Just three years after a World Championship, the Giants were a second division club and dead last in the National League in attendance.

But one could daydream. One could recollect. Let's take a step back.

The 1957 season felt like a season being played under water. The headlines about the move overshadowed everything on the ball field. Willie Mays had another fine year at the plate and led the league in triples. Johnny Antonelli led the pitching staff in wins and led the league in losses.

In June of 1957, the St. Louis Cardinals offered to send several players to New York plus $750,000 for Willie Mays. "Trader" Frank Lane couldn't control himself again, though he had created his own gap in center field by trading 1955 Rookie of the Year Bill Virdon to Pittsburgh for Bobby Del Greco.

The Giants didn't bite at Lane's offer. Musial's old buddy from the Cardinals, however, did land on his feet. On June 15, 1957 the New York Giants traded Red Schoendienst to the World Series-bound Milwaukee Braves in exchange for Danny O'Connell, Ray Crone and Bobby Thomson, the latter coming home as a hero, at least for a while.

Thomson would never play for the team in San Francisco. He would be dealt again to the Cubs the following spring, then play for the Red Sox and have a sip of coffee with the Orioles in 1961 before retiring. When the Giants left New York, Thomson had more home runs for the team than any player other than Mel Ott. Willie Mays was one home run behind him, one he would soon hit for the team in San Francisco. Eventually, Mays would be considered by some as perhaps the greatest player of all time, or perhaps second only to Ruth.

Soon after the second Schoendienst trade - the one that sent Red out to the dairy state Midwest to play near Mr. O'Malley's favorite new parking venue -the Brooklyn Dodgers and the New York Giants met for a final series at the Polo Grounds. The Dodgers won the first two, but the Giants won the third. Curt Barclay beat Don Drysdale, 3-2. A two-run home run by Hank Sauer, his 25th of the year, was the difference. The New York Giants won the lifetime series against the Brooklyn Dodgers, 650-606. The Giants had fifteen pennants and five World Championships in the modern era. The Dodgers had nine pennants and one World Series win. The balance would shift in the future.

Both teams were heading west, where the rivalry would continue and flourish. All of which, after seven and a half decades of baseball at a place known as the Polo Grounds, brought everyone to the bitter end.

So, for a final time, on September 29, 1957, the

Giants fans settled into a game at the Polo Grounds. The Pirates came to bat in the second inning.

It was difficult to fathom. Just three years after a World Championship, the Giants were last in the National League in attendance. One could daydream. One could recollect.

Memories were everywhere...

Several city blocks away, in a fading apartment on West 116th Street, an old man in his late eighties flipped the pages of a personal scrapbook as he watched the game on television. His name was Frederick Engel.

His hair was white. His health was fading, but the pictures in his scrapbook - the likenesses of Smilin' Mickey Welch, Orator Jim O'Rourke, and John Montgomery Ward - brought back his own memories.

Frederick Engel, called Freddy as a boy, had been the Giants' original mascot. But that was in a different time, way back seven decades earlier when his father, Nick Engel, operated the restaurant called The Old Home Plate. Back when men in tall hats and striped trousers watched the Giants play at 110th Street and Fifth Avenue, Freddy Engel had run messages from ballplayers to their lady friends. The scrapbook had been left to Engel by his father, who had died in 1897. For sixty years, the son had always cherished it.

Back at the ballpark, Frank Thomas of the Pirates homered off Antonelli to lead off the second. Roberto Clemente followed with a double. Antonelli hit Johnny Powers with a pitch. Hardy Peterson singled to right field, scoring Clemente from second. Bob Friend, the Pirate pitcher, singled to score Powers.

By the fourth inning, Antonelli was gone. Young Curt Barclay was pitching. The Bucs were leading 6-1. As the game continued and as the Giants' deficit mounted, the mood of the crowd darkened. In the top of the sixth inning, Ray Crone relieved Barclay. During the bottom of the inning, Rigney, a kind wise man who sensed the angry menace of the crowd, advised his players to sprint for the clubhouse at the game's conclusion.

"I told Mays not to worry about his hat or his glove," Rigney later recalled, "but about his life."

Watching the game from the dugout along with the players (and pictured here), was a sixteen-year-old boy named Eddie Logan, Jr. Eddie was the last New York Giants' batboy. Black and orange blood flowed through his veins. Eddie's grandfather, Fred Logan, was employed in the Giants' clubhouse in the late 1880s before later becoming clubhouse manager for both the Giants and Yankees in the 1920's. His father, Eddie Logan Sr., was the Giants' clubhouse manager in both New York and San Francisco.

Like Mays, Eddie received some good advice from a wise elder.

"Just before the last out, (Giants trainer) Doc Bowman said, 'Eddie, as soon as the last out is made, stay by me. Just stick by me. Take your cap off because we're going to run to the clubhouse. Be careful, because everybody is going to run on the field and the first thing they're going to want to do is steal your hat,'" Logan recalled many years later. "Sure enough, that's what happened. My father and grandfather were there all the time but they were never on the field. I was on the field for that one season."

{Author's note: Never underestimate a great batboy. Eddie Logan Jr. later became a Lt. Colonel in the United States Air Force.}

Stu Miller relieved Crone. Miller pitched the seventh and eighth.

In the top half of the ninth, Ramon Monzant relieved Miller. Monzant was a young Venezuelan who was the fleetest man afoot on the pitching staff. Johnny Powers capped a perfect day at the plate by hitting a blast over the right field roof, the last homer to be served up by New York Giants pitching in the Polo Grounds.

In the bottom of the ninth, Friend retired the first batter, Don Mueller, to fly out to right. That brought up Willie Mays, who already had two hits. Fans put their anger aside long enough to give Willie a Standing O. They begged for Willie to hit one out, pop one just one last time.

"The crowd was cheering so loud I felt helpless," he said later. "I got a home run my first time at bat in the Polo Grounds, and I wanted to bow out with another."

It was not to be. Mays bounced out to Dick Groat, the Pirate shortstop.

Dusty Rhodes prolonged things for a few minutes working to a full count. Then he broke his bat and knocked a weak ground ball to Groat. The surlier elements of the crowd started hopping over fences before Groat's throw reached Frank Thomas at first base.

It was 4:35 P.M., around the same time on a September afternoon - give or take a half an hour - as Thomson had homered.

Ugliness followed.

A significant element of the crowd pillaged the once majestic old park. The players from both teams fled immediately toward the weather-beaten center field clubhouse, some in real fear for their lives.

The first of the vandals cut second base loose from its moorings and then tossed it to a partner in crime to escape the groundkeepers. Some security people attempted to save the other two bases but were unsuccessful. Small crowds stood over home plate (where Ott used to dig in) and the pitcher's rubber (where Mathewson used to throw), eventually prying up both and absconding with them.

Invaders tore up the green canvas screen behind home plate. The bullpen shelters were smashed and splintered into portable pieces. Nothing vulnerable was untouched or undamaged. Driven by indignation, sorrow, and rage, the marauders went after everything.

The 483-foot sign in the deepest part of the ballpark was bent in half before security guards secured it. Thousands of others dug up sod or dirt. The heavy wooden seats, sturdy and bolted down, proved too stubborn. The most sacrilegious of the looters stole the center field plaque honoring Eddie Grant, the former Giant infielder who died in World War One. The other plaques were stolen also.

None was ever seen again.

"Thousands of fans responded to the final

melancholy out by chasing their California-bound idols to the clubhouse," wrote John Drebinger in The New York Times, "and carrying away everything on the field that could be moved. The mass pursuit was touched off by affection, excitement, nostalgia, curiosity and annoyance at the fact the team next year will represent San Francisco."

The image was that of a carcass being picked. It wasn't pretty. Some in the crowd chanted, "We want Stoneham, with a rope around his neck!"

"Only a witness to the Vandals' sacking of Rome in 455," wrote Steve Wulf in Sports Illustrated, many years later as he recalled the scene, "could do justice to a description of those frenzied minutes right after the game."

By quarter past 5 P.M, the darkness of evening approached. The pillaging subsided. Many fans congregated in front of the Giants' clubhouse. After taunting Stoneham, who was far away by this time, they pleaded to bid adieu personally to Willie Mays. Willie wisely declined to appear. Finally, turning angry again, the fans serenaded the Giants with some verses to the tune of The Farmer in the Dell:

"We hate to see you go,
"We hate to see you go,
"We hope to hell you never come back—
"We hate to see you go."
Really, it was horrible.

"I guess I'm dispossessed," said groundskeeper Matty Schwab, as he and his family relinquished their apartment under the left fiend grandstand.

"I played my first major league game here in 1946," Bill Rigney said to reporters. "And I can't tell you what a thrill it's been for me to put on the uniform in the same clubhouse that Matty and McGraw and Terry and Ott occupied."

By 5:30, a bittersweet calm had replaced the insanity on the field.

The Polo Grounds, what remained of it, was serene, though beaten up. Strains of *Auld Lang Syne*, drunkenly sung by the final guests who staggered out, echoed throughout.

On their way to the exit, Rigney and Giant vice-president Chub Feeney stopped to say goodbye to the members of the grounds crew who wouldn't be moving west to Seals Stadium.

Rigney told one of them, "I want to thank you guys for making this the best damn field..." Rigney began to one of them.

But he was too choked up to finish. He gave the man a hug and walked on. And he had been correct. It *had* been the best damned field.

Out on the diamond, with the crowd finally dispersed, between what remained of the first base line and the Giants' dugout, Bobby Thomson and his wife walked their daughter, five-year-old Nancy, to home plate. Her father recorded the scene with a home movie camera, the little girl happily circled the bases, shouting with happiness.

"Who knows?" said Bobby. "Maybe someday Nancy will have her own children. She can show them this movie and tell them about the home run that grandpa hit."

The old park would see major league baseball - or what occasionally passed for it - for two more years with the advent of the Mets in 1962 and 1963. At the time, a graceful New York essayist named Murray Kempton would write in *Sport Magazine* that the return of National League baseball to the old Polo Grounds was "like the raising of a sunken cathedral, its place sacred in history and hallowed in memory."

Absolutely correct.

But that would be five years in the future.

Today, everyone was looking backward, not forward.

Writer Roger Angell, on assignment from *Holiday* magazine, was there until the end. Mr. Angell was a long time Giants fan.

"I didn't feel anything," he would later write. "Nothing at all. I guess I just couldn't believe it. But it's true, all right. The flags are down, the lights in the temple are out, and the Harlem River flows lonely to the seas."

On September 29 there were only memories. And ghosts. As the afternoon died and you glanced around the old ballpark, you could see them, the ghosts, the memories in the autumnal shadows that deepened minute to minute.

There was the young John J. McGraw arriving from Baltimore, exorcising the demons of Andrew Freedman.. Christy Mathewson on the mound, young, handsome, gracious and gifted. Fred Merkle missing second, Rube Marquard winning nineteen in a row… McGraw furious as the White Sox won the 1917 World Series... Casey Stengel sitting on the bench with Mac, learning strategy… The men and women of Broadway. Cohan. Dauvray. Ida Schnall. Sinatra. Blossom Seeley… FDR watching the World Series. Mayors Jimmy Walker and Fiorello LaGuardia… Babe Ruth furiously barging into the Giant dressing room…

The ballpark as a backdrop of the racy wild limitless adventurous feel of Manhattan in the 1920's, when jazz was the soundtrack of the city and the liquor never stopped flowing despite Prohibition…the "constant flicker of men and women and machines," as F. Scott Fitzgerald wrote in *The Great Gatsby*…Bill Terry arriving from Louisiana. Then Carl Hubbell taking the mound with his bent left arm… Ott hitting 363 homers down the friendly right field line…

The international soccer.

The Gaelic soccer. Verdi.

The crazy little midget racers.

The great boxing.

The college and pro football.

The war years of the 1940's… The dim-outs… Leo

arriving belligerently from Brooklyn to take over his archrivals and guide them to pennants... Sal Maglie with a game-day scowl that could scare the Devil himself... The crisp white home uniforms with the black caps and the orange NY... Willie the Wonder, the ballplayer of a lifetime...

Johnny Mize...

Bobby Thomson... Monte Irvin... Dauntless Danny Gardella... Whitey Lockman... Hank Thompson... Antonelli... Jansen... Dusty Rhodes...

The New York Giants weren't dead, as Chuck Dressen twice suggested.

It was worse. They were gone.

Eventually, police cleared everyone from the old park. Mrs. John McGraw, still clutching her now-wilting roses, walked down the aisle toward an exit. Jane Mathewson was still conspicuous in her absence. Fifty years ago, when Jane's husband pitched for the Giants, she and Christy lived on Coogan's Bluff. She could see the scoreboard from her apartment window. When Christy was pitching, she could put a roast in the oven in the seventh inning and be certain that her husband would be home for dinner. Today, she lived far away and chose not to come. Too painful.

Officially, Blanche McGraw was the last Giants fan to leave.

She was helped to a car that would take her home to Pelham.

The gates clanked shut. They were padlocked.

"It would have broken John's heart," she said softly.

She was right. It would have.

"I've taken my boys to the house I grew up in. Taken them to the site of Ebbets Field, where the Dodgers used to play. They go to all the Dodger games, and they play Little League ball. I have infused them with New York spirit."

Larry King

*

"The Dodgers told me a big bonus was no good, and they said other players would resent it. Better for me to take a small amount of money and work my way."

Roberto Clemente

An Ebbets Field Reminiscence

My late mom, Shirley Sobel, was a diehard Dodger fan, so much so that she would con her friends into skipping school, Thomas Jefferson HS in East NY, to go to day games. She conned them into going by promising that she would take their swimming tests for them in gym if they accompanied her. Her friends couldn't swim, but mom was an accomplished swimmer and athlete.

They would hop on the IRT at New Lots Avenue and walk down from Eastern Parkway to get to Ebbets Field. They would watch the game from the cheap seats. Her first favorite player was Pete Reiser. Mom always said he would have been a HOF'er if he didn't crash into all those walls. When Jackie came on the scene she was 12 and that's when her crush on Reiser turned into true baseball love for # 42.

Her interest in the Dodgers totally consumed her. She suffered through all of the "wait till next year" seasons until 1955 when the Dodgers won it all. Both she and Jackie are linked eternally because both missed Game 7.

Jackie missed it due to injury and was replaced by Don Hoak. "Shirl" as we all called her, missed it because she had to go to Augusta, Georgia, to be with her husband, my dad, Morty Weiss, who was (in the US Army and) stationed in Ft. Benning.

Somehow she found a way to watch it on someone's black and white TV with fuzzy reception. Nobody understood why the Brooklyn girl with the heavy accent was screaming so loud that October afternoon, but she knew. When she finally got a phone line she called her parents (Mary and Harry Sobel) back home in East NY Brooklyn to cry and celebrate! Next Year had come!

I still love the Dodgers today thanks to my mom and my grandparents. The stories that they passed along to me made me love the Dodgers. I even went to Ebbets Field on the 50th Anniversary of the wrecking ball in order to pay homage to the boys of summer and my mom and grandparents.

I felt their presence while I was there in a very strange but emotional way.

Marc Weiss

Staten Island

September 2019

Seventh Inning Stretch, Chicago Style.

I offer you here a John Dillinger baseball card, "created" a few years ago by an inspired artist and designer named Gary Cieradkowski. If you Google

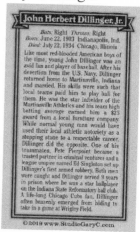

StudioGaryC.com you'll find and be able to purchase some wonderful stuff like this baseball card that he created.

Johnny Dillinger played minor league professional ball for a team in Martinsville, Indiana in 1924. Not long afterward he was lured into a local robbery by, of all people, a local umpire. He got busted and got his butt sent to a reformatory.

"(Dillinger)... quickly became the star ballplayer on the Indiana State Reformatory ball club," Gary Cieradkowski wrote recently. "He followed his Cubbies through the newspaper and took part in baseball betting pools. The constant denial of his parole eventually made him bitter. When he was transferred to the much harsher Indiana State Prison in Michigan City he convinced himself it was because the prison wanted him to play shortstop on their team..."

"The John Dillinger that emerged from prison in 1933 was now a well-educated criminal," Gary C continued. "He instantly embarked on a bank robbing tear that both shocked and fascinated the nation. Criss-crossing the country and living constantly on the run, Dillinger still took the time to follow the Cubs. In between robberies, he was said to have attended more than a few ballgames at Wrigley Field. In fact, before one game in August of 1933, the bank robber was pointed out to {former Brooklyn Dodger and then-Cub} outfielder Babe Herman as he sat with a group in the left field box seats. The Cubs great catcher Gabby Hartnett told how the Chicago police apparently knew about Dillinger's presence at Wrigley Field yet did nothing to turn him into the Feds."

Gabby Hartnett sure met some interesting folks playing in Chicago.

In September of 1933 Hartnett wandered over to the expensive seats at Comiskey Park to sign a baseball for a fan and his son. The fan was Al Capone and the boy was twelve-year-old Alphonse Jr., whom Dad called, Sonny. On the other side of Sonny, watching carefully, was Roland V. Libonati, a lawyer and then an Illinois state legislator, later elected to the US Congress from Illinois. The occasion was a charity game, Cubbies against Pale Hose, to raise money for the unemployed. Big Al had already financed several soup kitchens around Chicago, burnishing his Robin Hood image. Al had recently served a short jail sentence for carrying a concealed weapon. A few months later he would begin an eleven year prison sentence for tax evasion. He would serve eight years.

200

Check out the intimidating gentlemen in fedoras behind Scarface. Those are the boss's bodyguards and were not to be messed with. Look at the guy right behind Capone, identified by reports that day as "Machine Gun" Jack McGurn, who had been born in Sicily as Vincenzo Antonio Gibaldi. McGurn was a small time boxer, a night club owner and a Capone bodyguard. A vendor looks to have accidentally rubbed his shoulder and "Machine Gun" is either reaching for his wallet or is on alert to protect his boss. McGurn, alleged to be one of the planners of the infamous St. Valentine's Day Massacre was shot to death five years later at the second-floor Avenue Recreation Bowling Alley, at 805 N. Milwaukee Avenue in Chicago.

But on this afternoon in 1931 it was all father-and-son (plus the mouthpiece and three gunmen) and the enjoyment of a good baseball game. Harnett, who is smiling very politely in this photo, graciously signed a ball for Sonny. Wouldn't you do the same?

Commissioner Landis chewed out Gabby Hartnett after this photo and several others went public. The commish sent a message to the Cubbie catcher telling him to stop signing autographs for gangsters. Hartnett, who would end his career at the Polo Grounds with the New

York Giants in 1941, replied and told the commissioner that *he, the commissioner*, should tell the mob guys to stop asking if he felt so strongly about it.

This was Chicago after all and he was just trying to make nice with the hometown fans.

Check out Gary C's site, as mentioned. {**StudioGaryC.com**} He's got some great stuff. It's well worth a visit. Hint: Check out the "SHOP" for some great gifts for baseball fans.

Chapter 15 - The Making of Lake Candlestick

No story involving Candlestick Park, the home of the San Francisco Giants from 1960 until 2000, can begin or end without a discussion of the playing conditions. This chapter is no exception…and naturally the Dodgers are involved.

The dampness, the rain and particularly the wind became factors in any game at Candlestick as soon as the park opened. During an All Star game at Candlestick in 1961, a blast of wind prompted an umpiring decision that affected an All Star Game.

Stu Miller, all 165 pounds of him, was pitching in his home park in the ninth inning on July 11, 1961, when the steady breeze coming in off the Pacific Ocean decided to have some fun with the game in progress. There were runners on first and second and slugger Rocky Colavito was at the plate.

"Just as I was ready to pitch, an extra gust of wind came along, and I waved like a tree," Miller explained. "My whole body went back and forth about two or three inches. The American League bench hollered 'balk.' And I knew it was a balk. Colavito swung and missed. Then the umpire took off his mask and motioned the runners to second and third."

Obviously, the umpire, Stan Landes, hung onto his mask because otherwise it might have blown away. The inning proceeded. One run scored on an error by third baseman Ken Boyer. The run was charged to Sandy Koufax, whom Miller had relieved. That tied the score.

Miller surrendered another unearned run in the 10th inning. But Willie Mays doubled home Henry Aaron and scored a final run on a single by Roberto Clemente in the bottom of the 10th. The National League won, 5-4. Miller's consolation prize on the windiest of all All Star days was being the winning pitcher and known forever as the guy who was "blown off the mound" (not entirely accurate) by the Candlestick winds.

As years went by, there were other tales of terror by gale. One of the most memorable involved the headgear of former Cubs pitcher Ed Lynch, a thoughtful, intelligent man who later became the Chicago team's general manager.

Not only was Lynch's lid blown off his head, but it zipped all the way to the outfield wall and was held against the fence by the wind. That might not have been all that surprising, but the cap made it all the way to the fence without ever touching the grass.

Lynch, astonished, characterized the flight of his cap as "a frozen rope." Luckily it didn't kill someone in midflight. The weather at Candlestick, which included cold rain or even sleet from time to time, made Finland feel like Acapulco in comparison. Not only did it drive a generation of fans away from the ballpark, but it also drove otherwise rational fans to belligerent, borderline behavior.

Over the years, Matty Schwab - the same Matty Schwab who had been the head groundskeeper at New York's Polo Grounds - created an artistic montage on the wall in his office. It consisted of dangerous items hurled onto his field over the years by the lunatic fringe, made crazy presumably by the weather. The polar weather conditions also made Giants players cranky. Will Clark's voice was always alive with passion when he spoke about getting *Candlesticked,* a term that sounded like something out of a pornographic movie.

And Clark got to use the home dugout.

The Giants' dugout was heated, but the visitors' dugout was not. The Giants could also disappear down a corridor into the comparative warmth of their clubhouse, but the visitors – friends from other places like the L.A. Dodgers - had to walk across the field to get to their lockers. On the plus side, this perp walk provided certain visiting team members – we're thinking here of Tommy Lasorda, for example, whom Giant fans call 'Tommy Lasagna,' not that it's meant disrespectfully or anything - and Giants fans an opportunity, twice per game, to express their mutual admiration and love.

"Why was a major league park built here in the first place?" fans would often mutter.

While the question was rhetorical, and often included a few flourishes of profanity, there was an answer. The stadium site, situated at Candlestick Point on the western shore of the San Francisco Bay, was one of the few parcels of land available in the city that was suitable for a sports stadium and had space to park ten thousand cars. Parking was part of the bait that had been offered to Horace Stoneham to move the team from New York. Presumably an armada of cars were expected to come up out of the nearby ocean for home dates.

When Candlestick opened, in the first game on TV, which naturally had to be against the Dodgers, announcer Vin Scully gushed about the new ballpark. He cited its "radiant heating" piped into every seat. Great idea, but it never worked. San Francisco may have been a cool city, but Candlestick was cold. And windy. And wet. And frequently miserable.

This brings us to the latter stages the season that followed Stu Miller's rendez-vous with destiny on the pitcher's mound at The Stick.

1962.

Wouldn't you know it, the Giants and the Los Angeles Dodgers were locked cheek to jowl in yet another fierce pennant race. Enter two unlikely stars of the 1962 season: Giants head groundskeeper Matty Schwab, Jr., and his son, Jerry.

"I have to admit that it's a big thrill to have a packed stadium cheering your every move," recalled Jerry Schwab twenty-some years after the 1962 season. "It's fun to think back on what happened, to know that I did my part to get the San Francisco Giants into the World Series."

Schwab was speaking from his home in Florida, far from New York where he grew up and far from San Francisco where he took part in one of the most successful bits of sabotage ever performed on a baseball diamond.

We're talking now about the era of Marichal, Mays, Cepeda and McCovey. Schwab was twenty years old and couldn't run, throw or hit with any special skill. He wasn't even on the San Francisco roster. Nevertheless, he was a key player and made some critical moves on the base paths in the Giants' successful drive to the 1962 National League pennant.

The L.A. Dodgers were strong that year, led by Sandy Koufax, Don Drysdale, Junior Gilliam and Willie and Tommy Davis. But the real heart of the L.A. club was Maury Wills, the eventual MVP of the National League. Wills swiped everything but the pitchers' mail and the opposing players' wives and daughters that year. He was en route to erasing Ty Cobb's single-season theft record with 104 stolen bases, a record that was eventually swiped from him by Ricky Henderson with 130 steals in 1982.

In early August of 1962 the Dodgers — leading the second-place Giants by 5½ games —visited San Francisco for a three-game series. The Giants knew they would have to find a way to slow down L.A.'s running game, so before the series began, Giants manager Alvin Dark approached Matty Schwab, Jerry's father.

Matty was San Francisco's head groundskeeper and was so valuable and good at his job that, as noted, the team had brought Schwab with him from New York. {Readers of

an earlier chapter in this book will recall Matty and family
from the Polo Grounds, where they lived, and that before
coming to the Giants, in a wonderful bit of irony, Schwab
had been the groundskeeper at Ebbets Field.}

Al Dark had a key question for Schwab. Could
anything be done to keep the speedy Wills in check, Dark
asked.

Yes, Matty replied, he knew a trick or two. Things
could be arranged.

Monkeying with a playing field was nothing new,
but the trickery took ingenious new forms from season to
season. These days in the early 1960's there were some
interesting new spins.

The front, step-off portion of the pitcher's "mound"
at Crosley Field in Cincinnati, for example, was actually
dug out to create a concave effect, increasing the chances
of visiting pitchers' floating high, fat fastballs to Frank
Robinson, Wally Post and Gus Bell on the Reds' roster. The
baselines at Chicago's Comiskey Park were slanted toward
fair territory, the better to keep the bunts of home favorites
Luis Aparicio and Nellie Fox in play. Then, going back a
few years maybe, there were the outfield fences at
Municipal Stadium in Cleveland, which owner Bill Veeck
would regularly move *back* for the powerful Yankees and
in for the banjo-hitting St. Louis Browns.

Matty himself had no issues with tweaking the
Dodgers since he had seen the Dodgers' "1,000-pound
steam roller," a vehicle that looked suspiciously like those
used to flatten fresh asphalt on highways. Applied to the
outfield grass at Dodger Stadium, such a steam roller would
– in theory, at least - be a dandy way to stretch singles into
triples for a fast ball club.

Surprise, surprise! The Dodgers of 1962 tied for the
major league lead in triples. So when Dark asked Matty for
a little extra home-field edge against L.A., well, that was
what a good groundskeeper got paid for, right?

"Dad and I were out at Candlestick before dawn the day the series was to begin," Jerry remembered. "We were installing a speed trap."

Working with battery powered lanterns and flashlights, the Schwabs dug up and removed the topsoil where Wills would take his lead off first base. Down in its place went a squishy swamp of sand, peat moss and water. Then they cheerfully covered their chicanery with an inch of normal infield soil, making the 5-by-15-foot quagmire visually indistinguishable from the rest of the base path.

It was not so indistinguishable the next afternoon, however, as the Dodgers took batting practice. Leo Durocher, the L.A. third base coach at the time, and no stranger to a good on-field bitchfest, began digging it up with his cleats. Ron Fairly, the Dodger first baseman, called attention to it more artistically by building sandcastles near the bag.

All of this quickly caught the attention of umpire Tom Gorman.

Gorman, blessed with fine eyesight, could see that something unusual was lurking beneath the surface of the infield. He could also see that the entire Candlestick grounds crew had suddenly vanished when the Dodgers started scratching around. When Gorman finally found Matty Schwab, he threatened the Giants with a forfeit if the base paths weren't immediately repaired.

"Sure thing, Tom," said Matty, who was prepared for just such an ultimatum. "We wouldn't want a forfeit."

Out came the grounds crew. Up came some, but not all, of the Mystery Mixture. Away it was carted in wheelbarrows. Then, a few minutes later, back came more wheelbarrows to fill up the holes.

"It was the same stuff," Jerry said years later. "We mixed it with some dirt and brought it right back. When we put it down a second time it was even looser."

For some reason - exasperation, perhaps - this seemingly new concoction appeared to satisfy the umpires. Matty then ordered Jerry to water the infield, a task which Jerry performed generously and at length, much to the disgust of the Dodger dugout, from which derisive calls were emanating.

"What could you do?" remembered Tommy Davis, the 1962 batting champion and later a minor league hitting instructor for the Dodgers. "It was their park. They were going to get away with anything."

The Dodgers, robbed of their potent running game, stole no bases and went down to ignominious defeat, 11-2. The howls of protest from the L.A. side were heard all the way back to the National League headquarters in Cincinnati. There was even talk of digging up soil samples before the next game.

So out went the Schwabs, *père et fils*, before the next sunrise to remove the evidence. The next day the Dodgers looked hard for more dirty work, so to speak, but found none. What they did find was well-watered base paths, courtesy again of Jerry. So excessive was the moisture content of the base paths in Game 2 that the umpires stopped the game in midcourse and invited the Schwab gang to sand things down a bit, creating a nice marshy effect.

All this, needless to say, had a less than salutary effect on the Dodgers. Concerned about what to do **if** they got on base, the Dodgers forgot **how** to get on base. Wills, usually cool and collected, got himself tossed out of Game 2 by umpire Al Forman for arguing over how many times he had stepped out of the batter's box. The Dodgers lost that game 5-4 and the finale 5-1. They left San Francisco with their lead cut to just 2½ games.

Back in L.A., the local press was having a field day decrying the conditions up north in Baghdad on The Bay.

"They found two abalone under second base," wrote longtime Los Angeles *Times* columnist Jim Murray. Murray also suggested that an aircraft carrier could have safely navigated some of the deep infield waters.

Throughout Southern California, Al Dark - a nemesis to the Dodgers all the way back to Brooklyn days - became known as the Swamp Fox.

The Dodgers filed a complaint with the league office, just in case they should have to visit San Francisco for a playoff series after the regular season. National League president Warren Giles sent a letter to Giants president Horace Stoneham, mentioning Matty Schwab respectfully, but by name, growling about the field conditions. Stoneham passed the letter on to Matty, but conspicuously omitted any particular instructions for the future.

On the last day of the season San Francisco's Willie Mays crashed a home run to defeat Houston 2-1. Half an hour later, as the Giants sat huddled around a radio in their clubhouse, St. Louis beat the jittery Dodgers 1-0, leaving San Francisco and L.A. with identical 101-61 records for the regular season. A three-game playoff series was quickly scheduled, with the first game slated for Candlestick. The Schwabs had their cue to assemble the armada of wheelbarrows and get ready again with the Mystery Mixture.

"The only trouble was that [Hall of Fame umpire] Jocko Conlan arrived in San Francisco before we could do anything," recalled Jerry.

Indeed. Conlan took charge of the Candlestick turf before the Schwabs could lay a shovel on it. With the Dodgers due a few hours later, what were a loyal groundskeeper and his son to do?

The Schwabs decided that if the speed trap couldn't be hidden beneath the surface of the infield, they might just as well perform their antics openly. This time the Giants

210

grounds crew started by spreading sand generously around first base. When the Dodgers reported for practice, the infield was, in the words of The New York *Times*, "like a sandy beach well above the high water mark." There was no way anyone was going to get a firm foothold in that stuff.

"It's just as bad as the last time we were here, only in a different way," moaned Wills.

Jocko Conlan was not a happy man. He had prevented the Schwabs from digging, but the excessive sanding had gone on while his attention was elsewhere.

"Why don't you play the game like men?" he snapped angrily to Dark.

Close to game time, Conlan summoned Matty again and complained that the base paths were too dry and sandy. Schwab promised to take care of the problem right away. He summoned his waterman extraordinaire, Jerry.

"Get out there," he ordered, "and make a lake."

The large San Francisco crowd came alive as soon as Jerry appeared on the field with his hose. He watered the base paths as he normally would, then he watered them some more. He turned away, dampened the pitcher's mound, then returned to the base paths with a vengeance.

The result: Lake Candlestick.

The crowd loved it, howling their appreciation with every flourish of Jerry's hose.

"They were with me all the way, cheering me on," Jerry remembered. "I kept watering until the umpires came rushing over to stop me. Then I got out of there fast."

But the water, which was seen by the umpires as a means of slowing down the Dodgers, was actually only a clever ploy to force the umpires to order even more sand.

The ruse worked perfectly.

"What's all this mess?" one of the umpires rage to Matty.

"New man on the job," shrugged Matty. "We'll get this cleaned up right away!"

The "new man," it was noted, looked suspiciously like the same dude who had handled the hosing duties back in August. But before that realization could sink in, Matty was busy beckoning to his staff. Out came the wheelbarrows again and down onto those precious base paths went still more of the finest sand in northern California, creating a beachy effect. The only thing missing were surfboards and Dick Dale guitars, plus maybe Frankie and Annette.

The visitors stood helplessly in their dugout and watched. Again prevented from executing the style of baseball they favored, the Dodgers played in a trance all day. The Giants cruised to victory, 8-0, in the crucial first game.

The festivities moved to Los Angeles the next afternoon, where the Dodgers evened the series, 8-7. Back on the dry land of Dodger Stadium, Wills stole four bases in the final two games of the playoffs. Yet for all the shenanigans, it was an old-fashioned attack of wildness by the L.A. pitchers in the ninth inning of Game 3 that propelled San Francisco into its first World Series appearance. The Giants scored four in the ninth and left Dodger Stadium with a 6-4 victory.

Alas, the outcome of the Series was a familiar one, as the New York Yankees triumphed in seven games, a memorable series that ended with Willie McCovey lining a ninth inning two-on two-out laser shot toward right field that was intercepted by Yankee second baseman Bobby Richardson. In a final irony, the last two games in San Francisco were delayed by torrential rainstorms. The Schwabs were sent scurrying around the outfield spreading sand. Divine punishment, perhaps?

But, really, looking back on all this, a question persists: how did the Giants get away with such shenanigans?

Let's face it. To many people, San Francisco has always come off as a cool edgy place, or maybe just plain weird. A hundred and some years ago before the rise of Las Vegas and Los Angeles, the city named for the noble Saint Francis of Assisi was the Sin City of America: the gateway to the Pacific, the town of opium dens and Asian hookers, dice games with inebriated sailors and many equally select activities.

This is not an uncommon observation.

"What fetched me instantly (and thousands of other newcomers with me) was the subtle but unmistakable sense of escape from the United States," H.L. Mencken once wrote. And Herb Caen, the longtime columnist for the San Francisco *Chronicle*, once opined, "One day if I do go to heaven, I'll look around and say, 'It ain't bad, but it ain't San Francisco'."

In the mid-1950's, not long before the Giants moved to the bay, American kids learned about beat poetry by reading Lawrence Ferlinghetti and went on the road with Jack Kerouac. North Beach coffee houses were cool.

Many Americans were inspired in their motoring skills by Steve McQueen in *Bullitt*. They learned how to slap people around and irritate the boss by watching *Dirty Harry*. They learned how to zone out with the Grateful Dead and toke during the summer of love in Haight-Ashbury. The Hungry I, where Mort Sahl performed, was cool. Then there was a lady named Carol Doda, a stripper with forty-four inch breasts whose topless act debuted in San Francisco at the cheesy Condor Club. Later when the act wore a little thin, so to speak, Carol Doda upped the ante and continued to perform nude, paving the way for gentlemen's clubs in decades to come.

A quirky unique city. Yes, wonderfully so! Cool? Well, sometimes actually cold. Players wore heavy-duty sweatshirts and turtlenecks. The winds, which appeared to usually be hurricane force, comically whipped the players' baggy flannel pants.

What in the world does this have to do with baseball and the flooded base paths of 1962?

Simply this: San Francisco may have been a very cool place and a very beautiful place but Candlestick was a very cold place in a city that danced to its own beat. And in the haze of the years that have passed, it just may be that Giants' groundskeeping tactics in 1962 were inspired and facilitated by the anything-goes tone of the city as well as the bizarre-o weather conditions at the ballpark.

Playing conditions at the Stick were so aggrieved that they incubated a certain mindset. The umpires shrugged off the blatant sabotage that ensued as part of the climatic imposition facing all visitors to Candlestick. As Tommy Davis had said, what could you do?

As the years went by, Jerry Schwab, the one-time kid with the lethal hose, moved to Florida. He retained fond memories of his smooth play around the base paths. Matty Schwab retired and also moved to Florida, savoring an extraordinary career in the nuts and bolts of baseball

214

management, as well as the memory of the full share of
World Series loot that the Giants elected to give him.
      It was well earned.

*

**"Sometimes, sitting in the park with my boys, I imagine
myself back at Ebbets Field, a young girl once more in
the presence of my father, watching the players of my
youth on the grassy fields below—Jackie Robinson, Duke
Snider, Roy Campanella, Gil Hodges. There is magic in
these moments, for when I open my eyes and see my sons
in the place where my father once sat, I feel an invisible
bond among our three generations, an anchor of loyalty
and love linking my sons to the grandfather whose face
they have never seen but whose person they have come to
know through this most timeless of sports."**

Doris Kearns Goodwin
Wait Till Next Year

Chapter 16 – Because Many Brooklyn Fans Have Been Wondering…

Hilda Chester was the most famous Brooklyn Dodgers fan and possibly the most famous fan in baseball history before Jeffrey Maier and Steve Bartman - the latter duo having made the list for all the wrong reasons.

Hilda's long love for the Dodgers began as a teenager in the 1920's, when she loitered outside the offices of the Brooklyn *Chronicle* every day to hear the scores of the Dodgers' games. Eventually she scored passes to games from sportswriters. At one point, she was hired as a peanut sacker at Ebbets by the Harry M. Stevens corporation, which operated the concessions at all three New York ballparks. After she was done with her task of breaking down fifty pound sacks of peanuts into retail bags, she was able to watch the games. Eventually, she became a regular in the bleachers at Ebbets Field, but she was also known to follow the team to Philadelphia or to the Polo Grounds.

Thanks to her booming voice, resonant thick Brooklynese accent, distinctive print dresses, and fervent devotion to the Dodgers, Hilda became a celebrity throughout Brooklyn and beyond. She became even more famous after her first heart attack. Told by her physician not to yell anymore, she returned to Ebbets with a frying pan and iron ladle. The Dodgers' players soon replaced her noisemaking implements with a brass cowbell, which became her trademark, along with a bellowing, "Hilda is here," usually on arrival. No one ever accused Hilda of keeping her presence a secret.

Sometimes what she said had to be "interpreted" to tourists from other parts of the country. "Noive" meant "nerve," for example, "and "joik" meant "jerk." This was, after all, the borough where "tree doity boids" were "sittin' onda koib." When a Brooklyn newspaper's sports section proclaimed, "HOYT HURT" in advance of a World Series start many years ago, the news was locally pronounced, "HURT HOYT."

In 1941, Hilda suffered a second heart attack. Dodgers' manager Leo Durocher and several players visited her in the hospital. While Ebbets Field was notoriously hostile and difficult for visitors – a female fan once spit in Richie Ashburn's face, for example - Brooklyn was that sort of tight place for those who belonged there.

The Dodgers named their all-time team in between games of their Old Timers' Day doubleheader in 1955. On the occasion, they named Hilda as the Dodgers' greatest all-time fan. Really, no one could have been close.

Sadly, after the Dodgers moved to Los Angeles. Hilda Chester stated that she "wouldn't be caught dead" going to see them in Philadelphia, their closest stop to Brooklyn.

With her team gone, so was her grasp at stardom. A single woman with no immediate family, she remained a small time New York "personality" for several years. When Ebbets Field was torn down in 1960, she and five members of the Dodger Sym-Phony band appeared on *Be My Guest*, a television program that had a short run on CBS. Other guests included Ralph Branca and Carl Erskine.

Gradually, Hilda fell upon evil times. She sent occasional birthday cards to players from the old days, but then even those stopped. She became indigent and went into a nursing home. She died on December 1, 1978. She was buried in the Mount Richmond Cemetery on Staten Island by the Hebrew Free Burial Association.

There she lies today.

She does, however, still haunt the National Baseball Hall of Fame where a nearly life-size fabric-mâché statue of Hilda stands, oddly silent, cowbell in hand, clad in a print dress as usual. If you work it right, you can take a selfie with her. Many Dodger fans from the old days or their families come to the Hall of Fame and do exactly that. Hilda would have been pleased.

Happy Felton conducted the *Happy Felton's Knothole Gang* television show before Brooklyn Dodger baseball games and often did interviews with stars of a day's game after the last out. One of Mickey Mantle's strangest memories of playing against the Dodgers in the World Series was being led into a Brooklyn bar after certain games to be interviewed on Happy Felton's show. Enemy territory, indeed. The Mick had to push his way through muttering Dodger fans while still in uniform.

Happy Felton's real name was Francis J. Felton, Jr. He earned his nickname when he played Dr. Happy in a college dramatic production. His great desire in life was to be a baseball player, but he was always overweight. He was six feet tall but weighed 300 pounds at one time. In 1952 he was down to 275 but the avoirdupois kept coming back.

As a younger man, he led his own orchestra, playing at hotels and nightclubs across the United States. Eventually, he performed on Broadway, then met Walter O'Malley around 1950.

Mr. O'Malley, then vice president of the Dodgers, was intrigued with Felton's idea of running a TV program that would bring young fans to Ebbets Field for a pregame show with the players. Thus was born *Happy Felton's Knothole Gang.*

The show appeared on WOR TV, Channel 9 in New York, 25 minutes before home games at Ebbets Field. It usually featured three kids from local little leagues and a Dodger who gave them some brief baseball advice. Felton, amiable, pudgy and smiling, even with thick Phil Silvers-style glasses, would appear in a Dodger uniform and gently move things along. Often the show was on the air live from a remote area in foul territory at Ebbets Field. There were some live TV goofs and gaffes, too, which only made things more interesting. One time a kid begged to talk to Duke Snide who was in a terrible slump, having gone 0 for 21. It was never a top drawer idea to bring on a player who was slumping, but Snider agreed. Sure enough, when the kid got the Duke in front of a live camera he wouldn't shut up. "Gee, Duke," he said, "You *are* my idol, but this season you really stink!" Snider was shocked, then bemused,

220

chatted with the boy and snapped out of the slump shortly thereafter.

The production ran until the Dodgers left for California in 1958. Happy and his show were not invited to come along. In their new city, the Dodgers were anxious to shed their Brooklyn past.

Felton continued to work as an actor and via personal appearances based on his Dodger persona. But health problems emerged, most likely due to the ravages of being overweight. He lived on East 72nd Street in Manhattan and died on October 21, 1964, at Mount Sinai Hospital, also in Manhattan. He was a good man but he left us far too early; he was only 57.

Emmett Kelly was the sad faced clown who worked as the mascot for the Brooklyn Dodgers in 1956. Originally an American circus performer, he created the memorable tragic clown figure "Weary Willie" based on the hobos of the Depression era. He worked for various American circuses for most of his life, but it took more than a decade to get approval to use the sad clown act. Before that, Kelly was a high flying trapeze artist, usually working without a net.

Sports cartoonist William Mullin, who drew daily for The New York *World Telegram and Sun* sketched an image of Kelly's character to represent the Brooklyn Dodgers as "Dem Bums" in the 1930's. The character, who spoke an exaggerated Brooklynese, caught on with Dodger fans. Mullin illustrated the covers of team yearbooks with variations of the "Brooklyn Bum" for years afterwards, a spin on the Weary Willy image.

Emmett Kelly from Kansas was famous long before he was hired by the Brooklyn Dodgers. He was a cartoonist who later became a clown. Before coming to Ebbets Field he had been performing in circuses for decades. In 1942, he joined the Ringling Brothers and Barnum & Bailey Circus and established his place in the pantheon of American bit top performers. Willie wore a dirty derby, rags, and had a frown painted on an unshaven face.

"Weary Willie…always gets the short end of the stick and never has any luck, but he never loses hope and keeps on trying," Kelly used to explain. For the America that lived through the Great Depression, this persona resonated. Willie became an icon. World famous. Loren MacIver, the influential American painter and the first woman represented in the Museum of Modern Art's permanent collection, painted his portrait. He once met Winston Churchill because Churchill wished to meet Kelly.

The infamous Hartford (Connecticut) Circus Fire took place during an afternoon show on July 6, 1944. The tent and bleachers caught fire and the site became an inferno. The fire began near the main entrance and there was no emergency escape route for those inside. In ten minutes, one hundred sixty-seven people died, most of them burned alive. Nearly seven hundred were injured. No cause was ever established but a careless cigarette was frequently blamed.

Kelly was so traumatized by the event that he could never remember where he was when the fire began.

Wherever he was, Kelly acted quickly. He picked a bucket of water, probably the one he used to wash his makeup off after performances and rushed through the hysteria toward the blaze, not yet aware of its immense scope.

A circus attendee named Ralph Emerson snapped a photo of him in full stride, the famous sad clown rushing to help, carrying a bucket which would be useless against a blaze that is incinerating everything in its path. Later, Kelly pulled up the canvas of the tent and enabled dozens of panicked children to escape. It was wartime. The crowd was mostly women and children. Kelly was a quoted in numerous accounts of having screamed to separated mothers and children, "Keep moving! You can't get back in there!"

Emerson's picture was seen around the world, along with others of Kelly in tears after the fire. Because of the photo of Kelly, the day would later be known as "the day the clown cried."

A myth emerged: ever afterwards whenever Emmett Kelly appeared as Weary Willie, a small tear could be seen on his left cheek. Kelly painted it on, the myth went, in honor of the nearly nine hundred Hartford victims. This myth was just that: a myth. What was true was that Emmett Kelly never shook the horror of the fire. He said it was like a movie playing on a single reel, repeating every day forever.

Weary Willie's famous schtick was to sweep up the circus rings after the other performers. He would try and fail to sweep up a circle of light of a spotlight. His routine was revolutionary, as was the bittersweet sad clown persona. The link between Kelly and his clown character and the Brooklyn team was perhaps inevitable, given its origin. But it didn't last long and it was not the type of urban tragic act that Dodger management wished to transplant to sunny surfy California.

Emmett Kelly died of a heart attack at age eighty while taking out his garbage on March 28, 1979. He was at his home in Sarasota, Florida. There is no question in the minds of those who knew him that an image of Hartford in 1944 was probably playing in Kelly's head when he drew his last breath.

Kelly was an inaugural inductee to the International Clown Hall of Fame in 1989. He was inducted into the International Circus Hall of Fame in 1994. Largely forgotten today to those too young to personally remember him, he was a man of great character and compassion and an American performer of enormous and unique stature.

Gladys Goodding, the lady who played the organ for decades and sang *The Star Spangled Banner* in a soaring ethereal soprano – some who remember her insist she was a contralto - voice at Ebbets Field, was not a native New Yorker. But she should have been. She was born in Missouri and learned music from her mother, a music teacher. Both parents died prematurely. She spent a large part of her childhood in an orphanage in St. Louis.

As a young adult, she began performing light opera and musical theater through the American midwest. She married and had two children. She divorced in 1923 and moved to New York.

Music remained her livelihood. She played organ and piano at silent movie theatres in the Loews chain and performed on radio and in orchestras.

She played the organ at hockey and boxing at Madison Square Garden, then eventually basketball. In 1942, the Dodgers installed a permanent organ at Ebbets Field. Gladys heard about this and wrote to Larry McPhail (who was running the Dodgers at the time) telling him that he needed a full time keyboard player at his ballpark and she was the one he should hire. He heard her play and agreed.

Fans took to her immediately. Gladys Goodding was part of the soundtrack of Ebbets Field - much like a bat hitting a pitch, or a ball smacking into a leather glove, or the boo birds in the grandstand, the vendors in the narrow aisles, or Hilda Chester's leather-lunged voice and rattling cowbell, or Tex Rickards' avuncular malapropisms.

In 1947, she wrote and recorded *Follow the Dodgers*, which became the team's theme song. Over the years, she won the hearts of Dodger fans with her amusing and sometimes not so subtle musical commentary of events on the field. When the Dodgers lost the seventh game of the 1952 World Series at Ebbets, for example, blowing a game that many people thought they should have won, Gladys played, *What Can I Say After I Say I'm Sorry?*

Her mastery of her Hammond organ was total. Her knowledge of all types of music was exhaustive. Her "organ loft" high above the first base side was her command post from which she could survey the game in progress.

She introduced Mexican music and culture into the spirit of Ebbets Field. Her live organ renditions of *Las Chiapanecas* - a traditional Mexican melody from the state of Chiapas - became central to the seventh inning stretch at

Ebbets, during which the rhythmic clapping of fans and stomping of feet would punctuate Gladys' solo organ music. It spread to numerous other sports venues around the United States.

She knew all the players. They knew her. If a Dodger was celebrating a birthday, Gladys would play *Happy Birthday*. At other times, she would play a state song for a player or a favorite pop tune.

Not everyone was a fan, especially when games at Ebbets Field went late into the evening. She was once hauled into court by a cantankerous resident of the Ebbets neighborhood who alleged the organ music was interfering with his sleep. The judge dismissed the case when the plaintiff had to cup his hands behind his ears to hear the judge's questions.

At another time, a three man umpire crew was less than happy with Gladys' rendition of *Three Blind Mice* when they emerged from the dugout before the game. She later apologized to the men in blue and the apology was accepted.

She remained in New York after the team left, most prominently playing at Madison Square Garden. She lived at the Belvedere Hotel on West 48th Street, not far from the Garden. She died suddenly of a heart attack on November

16, 1963, a few days after working a Knicks game. She was seventy years old.

Her gorgeous voice will never be silenced. Her recordings of the National Anthem as she passionately sang it and played it at Ebbets Field remain on *MLB.com* and *You.Tube* among other web sites. You can listen to her right now.

Ebbets Field stood for another two and a half years after Dee Fondy of the Pirates grounded out to shortstop to end the game on September 24, 1957. But with that putout, Ebbets Field closed forever to major league baseball. There were various plans to save the old ballpark, but there had also been various plans to keep the Dodgers in Brooklyn.

Nothing came to serious fruition.

In the final two years of the 1950's, there was high school and college baseball, pro soccer from Europe and the United States and a few isolated other events - such as Demolition Derbies - at Ebbets Field. One of the demolition derbies tore up the grass so badly that some fans who had taken kids, just to show them the old park, left in tears.

One gentleman who tried to do right by his old ballpark was Roy Campanella.

His health was frail after his devastating car accident in 1957, but he still had some business interests in New York. He attended spring training at Vero Beach in 1959 and went out to Los Angeles for the big night in his honor at the Coliseum on May 7, 1959. He appeared amidst the sulkies and railbirds at Yonkers Raceway on July 1. In August, he appeared on an episode of the TV show, *Lassie*.

Campy lured a ragtag collection of Negro League teams and stars - fighting against the calendar and the tide of history - into playing a few games at Ebbets. Eight games on four dates were played in July and August 1959.

On August 23, 1959, Satchel Paige was the main attraction in a doubleheader that drew 4,000 fans. Paige admitted his age to be "somewhere between 40 and 60." That was true. He was actually 53.

Satch's squad topped the Campanella Stars 3-1 in the opener. Satch wore a Chicago White Sox uniform lent to him by Bill Veeck and fanned four in a three-inning start. He yielded a homer when he got cute and tried to sneak a second blooper pitch by Monarchs player-manager Herm Green. In all, Paige allowed three runs, but only one was earned.

There was a fine composer and songwriter named Joe Raposo whose best work was done in the middle of the Twentieth Century. His best known compositions were on *Sesame Street*. He wrote the theme song as well as classics such as *Bein' Green* and *C Is For Cookie*. Joe wasn't a Brooklyn guy; he was originally from Fall River, Massachusetts. But he was a smart man and knew a thing or two about life. He also knew Frank Sinatra. He and Frank were friends.

In the early 1970's, Raposo wrote a great song for Sinatra's 1973 comeback album titled *,Ol' Blue Eyes is Back*. It was called *There Used to Be a Ballpark*.

You know the song. You know the sentiment.

The lyrics convey the sadness at the loss of a baseball team and its ballpark, which once gave happiness and community to its fans and players. There's a particularly poignant line that goes:

> *Now the children try to find it*
> *And they can't believe their eyes*
> *For the old team just isn't playing...*

Raposo, who died at age 51 in 1989 of non-Hodgkin's lymphoma, frequently said that the song was about the Polo Grounds, where the New York Giants had played until departing with the Dodgers after the 1957 season. But he also wrote in his memoirs that he once went to Flatbush with writer Pete Hamill to research material for a television show. They went to the Ebbets Field housing project where, irony of ironies, they spotted a sign which read:

No Ball Playing Allowed

Thus the song can be heard as an ode to the loss of any ballpark, or even a larger loss: neighborhood, love, community, youth.

"The summer," the song says, "went so quickly this year." Summers do that. They go by quickly. But in associating the song with Ebbets Field, the poignancy is particularly intense. For kids who grew up in the vicinity of Ebbets Field, the Dodgers' presence there has been reduced to one long enticing summer day of youth. Now it's long gone, along with cherished parents, siblings, friends and neighbors.

The demolition of Ebbets Field began on February 23, 1960. Someone with a lousy sense of humor painted a baseball design onto a wrecking ball. The walls started to come down. About four hundred people came out to watch… and in some cases weep.

Tex Rickards was there to introduce some of the former players in attendance. One player was Ralph Branca. When Tex introduced him, he gave Branca's number as "fourteen." Ralph wore thirteen. Loveable Tex was gaffe-prone not just till the end, but beyond the end. Always that fifty-fifty chance of getting it right. And even today, the fans would have it no other way.

Campy was the guest of honor, a dubious distinction. He was in his wheelchair. Friends presented him with his old locker and his old uniform, with the big *39* on the back. Carl Erskine was there, ever classy, ever popular. So was Tommy Holmes, a born-in-Brooklyn guy who played for the Boston Braves and did a final year cameo as a pinch hitter in 1952. He was on the field when the Yankees won the World Series against Brooklyn that year.

Remember Otto Miller, who was the catcher in the first game on April 19, 1913? The guy who was also on the butt-end of the Wambsganss triple play in the 1920 World Series? The most famous Dodger most people have forgotten? The guy you never heard of till you read this book?

Otto was there. "I remember the first game well," he said. "Philadelphia beat us, 1-0."

Us.

Us. At heart, Otto was still a Brooklyn Dodger, now at age seventy-one. He was older than the ballpark.

When all the solemn words were over, the big wrecking ball came down and smashed the visiting team's dugout, the place where the Giants and Yankees used to sit, plus all those other National League visitors: the Braves, the Reds, the Cardinals, the Phillies, the Cubs and the Pirates.

And so an era ended, not necessarily replaced by something better.

Seats from the wreckage were sold for five bucks and pieces of sod for two bits. The flagpole located in centerfield went to a company in Flatlands, New York. Ebbets Field's cornerstone and other artifacts escaped to the Baseball Hall of Fame. They can be found not far from Hilda Chester's fabric mâché likeness.

An apartment complex was built after the demolition of Ebbets Field. A plaque commemorates the ballpark's past. Most residents are oblivious of the field's history.

Beyond that, almost everything and everyone is gone, aside from the memories.

Bedford Avenue and Sullivan Place, Brooklyn. USA.

There used to be a ballpark here.

THE END

Feedback

Readers can reach Noel Hynd at Nh1212f@yahoo.com. Readers are invited to communicate with any comments, observations or possible corrections. I'm happy to hear from you. Reviews on Amazon.com are greatly appreciated also.

Acknowledgements

Photographs

All photographs are either public domain or Creative Commons or "Fair Usage" unless otherwise indicated. Sometimes the rights to specific prints have become muddled over the years. If an unknown photographer covered a ball game in 1942 and turned his work over to a newspaper that no longer exists, who owns the rights today, for example? Generally speaking, American photos from 1928 or before are now in the public domain, as are many in the decades that followed where rights were never claimed or renewed. Bowman baseball cards, for example, never renewed their copyrights. Some photographs are in the public domain in the United States because they were published in the United States between 1923 and 1977 without a copyright notice. Publicity shots of film stars, theater and tv stars baseball stars were frequently in this category. The most recent photo or illustration used here is from 1957, aside from photos [provided with personal anecdotes.] I've done my best to track down rights and attribute them here. In the odd event that something here has been used without proper permission, please contact me at Nh1212f@yahoo.com.

Bibliography

Alexander, Charles C., *Ty Cobb*. New York: Oxford Univ. Press, 1984.
Allen, Lee. *The National League Story*. New York: Hill & Wang, 1961.
--. *The World Series*. New York: Putnam, 1969.

Appel, Marty, *Casey Stengel: Baseball's Greatest Character*, Doubleday, New York, 2017

Baldassaro, Lawrence, *Beyond DiMaggio*, U of Nebraska Press, Lincoln, Nebraska, 2011

Bevis, Charlie, *Sunday Baseball*, McFarland and Company, 2003

Cohen, Richard M., and David S. Neft. *The World Series.* New York: Macmillan, 1986.

Connor, Anthony J. *Voices from Cooperstown.* New York: Macmillan, 1982.

Creamer, Robert W. *Babe: The Legend Comes to Life.* New York: Simon & Schuster, 1974.

--.   *Stengel: His Life and Times.* New York: Simon & Schuster, 1984. Daley, Arthur. *Sports of the Times.* New York: Dutton, 1959.

Dickey, Glenn. *The History of the World Series Since 1903.* New York: Stein & Day, 1984.

Durocher, Leo. *Nice Guys Finish Last.* New York: Simon & Schuster, 1975.

Durso, Joseph. *The Days of Mr. McGraw.* Englewood Cliffs, N. J.: Prentice-Hall, 1969.

Einstein, Charles, ed. *The Baseball Reader.* New York: Harper & Row, 1980.

Fair, James, *Give Him To The Angels*, -, 1946 (Republished by Summersdale Publishers, 1997)

Fitzgerald, F. Scott, *The Great Gatsby*, Charles Scribner's, New York, 1925

Fleming, Gordon H. *The Dizziest Season.* New York: Morrow, 1984.

--.   *The Unforgettable Season.* New York: Holt, Rinehart & Winston, 1981.

Frommer, Harvey. *New York City Baseball.* New York: Macmillan, 1980.

Gehrig, Eleanor, and Joseph Durso. *My Luke and I.* New York: Crowell, 1976.

Golenbock, Peter. *Bums: An Oral History of the Brooklyn Dodgers,* New York: Putnam, 1984.

Goodwin, Doris Kearns, *Wait Till Next Year*, Simon and Schuster New York 2009

Graham, Frank. *McGraw of the Giants.* New York: Putnam, 1944. Goldstein, Richard. *Spartan Seasons.* New York: Macmillan, 1980. Honig, Donald. *The National League.* New York: Crown, 1983.

Heller, Peter, *In This Corner*, Da Capo Press, New York, 1994

Hynd, Noel, *The Giants of The Polo Grounds*, Doubleday & Company, New York 1988 and Red Cat Tales Publishing (Revised Expanded Edition, Los Angeles, 2018)

Jennison, Christopher. *Wait 'Til Next Year.* New York: Norton, 1974.

Joyner, Ronnie. *Hardball Legends and Journeymen*, McFarland & Company, Jefferson, N.C. and London, 2012

Kahn, Roger. *The Boys of Summer.* New York: Harper & Row, 1972. Kiernan, Thomas. *The Miracle at Coogan's Bluff.* New York: Crowell, 1975.

King, Joe. *The San Francisco Giants.* Englewood Cliffs, N. J.: Prentice- Hall, 1958.

Levine, Peter. *A. G. Spalding and the Rise of Baseball.* New York: Oxford Univ. Press, 1985.

- , Ellis Island to Ebbets Field. New York, Oxford, 1993

Lieb, Fred. *Baseball as I Have Known It.* New York: Coward, McCann & Geoghegan, 1977.

Mack, Connie. *My Sixty-six Years in the Big Leagues.* Philadelphia: Winston, 1950.

Mathewson, Christy. *Pitching in a Pinch.* New York: Putnam, 1912.

McGee, *The Greatest Ballpark Ever*, Rivergate Books, New Brunswick, NJ, 2005

McGraw, John J. *My Thirty Years in Baseball.* New York: Boni & Liveright, 1923.

McGraw, Mrs. John J. *The Real McGraw.* New York: D. McKay, 1953.

Mead, William B. *Even the Browns.* New York: Contemporary Bks., 1978.

Meany, Tom. *Baseball's Greatest Teams.* New York: A. S. Barnes, 1949. Morris, Lloyd. *Incredible New York.* New York: Random House, 1951.

Morris, Peter, A *Game of Inches: The Stories Behind the Innovations That Shaped Baseball*, Ivan Dee, Chicago, 2006, 2010

Neft, David, Cohen, Richard and Korch, Rick, in *The Complete History of Professional Football from 1892 to the Present,* St. Martin's, New York, 1994

The Ultimate Baseball Book. Okrent, Daniel, and Harris Lewine, eds.
Boston: Houghton Mifflin, 1979.

Nelson, Kevin. *Baseball's Greatest Quotes.* New York: Simon & Schuster, 1982.

New York Giants Yearbook(s), Big League Books, New York, 1951-57

Peterson, Robert. *Only the Ball Was White.* Englewood Cliffs, N.J.: Prentice-Hall, 1970.

Reichler, Joseph L. *The Baseball Trade Register.* New York: Macmillan, 1984.

Ed., The Baseball Encyclopedia. New York: Macmillan, 1982, 1984.

Reidenbaugh, Lowell. *Cooperstown.* Norwalk, Conn.: Arlington House, 1986.

--.   *Take Me Out to the Ball Park.* St. Louis: *The Sporting News*, 1983.

Ritter, Lawrence. *The Glory of Their Times.* New York: Macmillan, 1966.

Robinson, Ray, Matty: An American Hero, Oxford University Press, NY, 1993

Rust, Art, Jr., with Edna Rust. *Recollections of a Baseball Junkie.* New York: Morrow, 1985.

Seymour, Harold. *Baseball: The Early Years.* New York: Oxford Univ. Press, 1960.

Smith, Kenneth. *Baseball Hall of Fame.* New York: A. S. Barnes, 1952. Smith, Robert. *World Series.* Garden City, New York: Doubleday, 1967.

Stein, Fred. *Under Coogan Bluff.* Glenshaw, Pa.: Chapter & Cask, 1978.

Stein, Fred, and Nick Peters. *Giants Diary.* Berkeley, Cal.: North Atlantic Books. 1987.

Threston, Christopher. *The Integration of Baseball in Philadelphia*. McFarland, Jefferson, N.C.

Thorn, John. *A Century of Baseball Lore*. Hart Publishing New York, 1983

---, *Baseball in the Garden of Eden: The Secret History of the Early Game,* Simon and Schuster, New York, 2012

Van Hyning, Thomas. E., *Puerto Rico's Winter League: A History of Major League Baseball's Launching Pad*. Jefferson, North Carolina: McFarland & Co., 1995.

--- *The Santurce Crabbers: Sixty Seasons of Puerto Rican Winter League Baseball*. Jefferson, North Carolina: McFarland & Co., 1999.

Weintraub, Robert, The Victory Season, Little Brown, Boston, 2013

Zang, David, *Fleet Walker's Divided Heart: The Life of Baseball's First Black Major Leaguer,* Legacy Audio Books, 2007

Periodicals and Online Sources

New York *Times*, New York *News*, Boston *Globe*, The Philadelphia *Inquirer*, *The Sporting New*s, The Brooklyn *Eagle*, *The Wall Street Journal*, The Chicago *Sun*, *Variety*, *The Morning Telegraph*, The Chicago *Sun*. I am particularly indebted to a New York *Times* article titled *Presidents Who Knew the Babe* - The New York *Times*, April 11, 2015. Similarly, I acknowledge the helpfulness of an article titled, *A flood of memories of 'Stick in '62* by Scott Ostler in December 20, 2013 | Scott Ostler.

Wikipedia

The Ring Magazine

Baseball Almanac: Baseball History, Baseball Records and Baseball at www.baseball-almanac.com

http://www.baseballinwartime.com

I used Baseball Reference (https://www.baseball-reference.com) as my source for statistics. Thank you BB-Reffy for all those beautiful numbers.

Special Mention - **SABR**

I used SABR (Society for American Baseball Research) extensively for this book and my book, *The Giants of The Polo Grounds*.

The site is https://sabr.org.

I gratefully acknowledge use of SABR's site and the work of countless SABR historians. I am specifically indebted to SABR's researchers on the following players, with the researcher acknowledged in parentheses after the player's name. **Thank you**, men and women of SABR.

In random order: Sal Maglie (**Judith Testa**), Leo Durocher (**Jeffrey Marlett**), Bill Rigney (**Alan Cohen**), Rube Marquard (**Joseph Wancho**), John McGraw (**Don Jensen**), Christy Mathewson (**Eddie Frierson**), Bill Terry (**Fred Stein**), Willy Mays (**John Saccoman**), Monte Irvin (**Larry Hogan**), Ebbets Field (**Rory Costello and Bob McGee**), Duke Snider (**Warren Jacobs**) Danny Gardella (**Charlie Weatherby**), Danny Litwhiler (**Glen Vasey**), Bobby Thomson (**Jeff Findley**), Hugh Mulcahy (**C. Paul Rogers III**), Sid Gordon (**Ralph Berger**), Happy Felton (**Rob Edelman**), Jack 'Lucky' Lohrke (**Andy Sturgill**), Wilbert Robinson (**Alex Semchuck**), Johnny Antonelli (**Alexander Edelman**), Jack Chesbro (**Wayne McElreavy**), Moonlight Graham (**Jimmy Keenan**), Mike "Pinky" Higgins (**Mark Armour**), Al Brazle (**Gregory H. Wolf**), Ruben Gomez (**Thomas Van Hyning**), Lee Grissom (**Charles F. Faber**)

Noel Hynd is the author of several highly successful political thrillers such as *Firebird* and *Flowers From Berlin* as well as several supernatural thrillers such as *Ghosts* and *Cemetery of Angels*. He is a graduate of the University of Pennsylvania and a former contributor to *Sports Illustrated.*

Final Thought

"If you don't love the Dodgers, there's a good chance you may not get into Heaven."

Tommy Lasorda

The Final Game at Ebbets Field   Noel Hynd

Made in the USA
Monee, IL
30 October 2020

46426243R00141